TALKING ABOUT PSYCHICAL RESEARCH

THOUGHTS ON LIFE, DEATH AND THE NATURE OF REALITY

TALKING ABOUT PSYCHICAL RESEARCH

THOUGHTS ON LIFE, DEATH AND THE NATURE OF REALITY

BY

MARY ROSE BARRINGTON

www.whitecrowbooks.com

PRAISE FOR

TALKING ABOUT PSYCHICAL RESEARCH

~

"Having attended many of Ms Barrington's psychical research lectures, I am delighted that she has finally put them down on paper in this book. The reader is presented with several decades of serious research, personal experience, and classic scholarship, which cannot be bought, and is only down to the dedication and commitment she has given to psychical research. A valuable insight!"

~ **CALLUM E. COOPER, PhD,** UNIVERSITY OF NORTHAMPTON, CO-EDITOR OF *PARACOUSTICS: SOUND & THE PARANORMAL*

"This witty and perceptive collection of essays is the harvest of sixty years of active membership of The Society for Psychical Research.

Combined with a legal background, Ms Barrington achieves an exceptional analysis and penetration of a wide variety of incidents, experiences and concepts that are associated with paranormal phenomena (which are, she points out, normal for many people).

Her book, *Talking about Psychical Research: Thoughts on Life, Death and the Nature of Reality* prompts thinking about psychical research in a critical yet constructive way. Even when she discusses well-known cases and re-occurring philosophical problems, there is a freshness of treatment that leads to new interest and insights. From the rich mix of life experiences and thinking that forms the content of psychical research, Ms Barrington has put together a collection that underlines the substance and importance of this field of study, and develops a "mind infused", multi-level worldview to accommodate psychic phenomena.

This collection deserves a place on the bookshelf of anyone interested pondering over the field and its history".

~ **JOHN POYNTON,** PAST PRESIDENT OF THE SOCIETY FOR PSYCHICAL RESEARCH

CONTENTS

～

FOREWORD

~

For those of us who are seasoned travellers in the field of psychical research, this book offers a fascinating overview of the author's contribution to it, leading to conclusions that require and inspire some profound reflection. Those who are starting out on the journey could not ask for a guide that was more companionable, informative, or better at putting you at ease than Mary Rose Barrington. That was what she did for me when I met her many years ago, attending a Society for Psychical Research Study Day for the first time. Since then we have been companions in exploration of that most challenging field, psychical research, and for me it has been a most rewarding personal experience.

And it is personal experience that is at the heart of this book, experience understood in its wider philosophical sense, not only as the basis of psychical research but, at its deepest level, of human life itself. Some philosophies disparage that experience as just stories that we weave about ourselves; often it is dismissed as "anecdotal" as opposed to "scientific" evidence, but this book starts from the acceptance of "anecdotes" (and that includes accounts of scientific experiments!) as fundamental to our experience of the world. That means examining all "anecdotes" for which there is good evidence, not just those aspects of experience which fit in with how we currently think the world works. It also means disregarding the various boggle-thresholds which hold back many of us, parapsychologists and psychical researchers included, from examining the evidence of psychical research in its totality. Taking such a wide-lens view leads to the conclusion that psychical research is "the study of unpredictable events and uncontrollable effects", beyond the reach of current scientific methodology "because they are outside sequential causality". Thus attempts to make psi phenomena fall into line by trying to replicate them hard enough and for long enough are always going to miss the point. Instead, we should see psychical research as a "chronicle of non-conforming facts", and accept psi phenomena on their own terms. This does not give up on rationality, but means observing with care and attention, and going where the evidence leads and not trimming it into shapes that fit our frameworks. It also provides a persuasive argument for the view that it is natural for psi to be elusive.

In fact, some of these "unpredictable events and uncontrollable effects" pursued by psychical research may be more common than we think; however, they pass unnoticed among incidents usually put down to inattention and malobservation. Jotts (acronym of "just one of those things") is the name used for articles which, among other things, go missing, turn up again in faraway places, or return in a modified form. The author can justifiably take the credit for identifying these events as a separate phenomenon, since she has been collecting, sifting and classifying authentic cases of "spatial discontinuity" for some 30 years. They may sound trivial, but many of the cases quoted here, and described at greater length in her book devoted to the phenomenon (Barrington 2018), are difficult to dismiss as due to "natural" causes. If you examine the evidence of centuries of poltergeist cases, where objects materialise suddenly out of nowhere, relocate and travel along impossible trajectories, there is a logical as well as evidential argument for suspecting that the less conspicuous events, such as jotts, are psi phenomena that are simply not different enough from ordinary life, not noticeable enough to draw our attention. But then you have to go further, to the mind-boggling but well documented phenomena of physical mediumship, where "the physical environment loses its causal fixity and becomes plastic, letting itself be moulded by the mindpower of participants in a highly deviant reality."

What this mindpower is, and how it produces the "psychic force" that draws together mental and physical psi phenomena, is one of the questions that the book's "small theory of everything" explores. Ideas about the role of the mind in determining the nature of reality have recently been making their cautious way into the mainstream in discussions about consciousness and information. Here, however, we deal with the full spectrum of psi phenomena, as well as the maintenance of the structure of ordinary reality, with probability assigned a special role. Large philosophical ideas emerge from modest little jotts, poltergeist phenomena, healing, telepathy, the clairvoyance of psi virtuosi such as Didier and Ossowiecki, and evidence of survival of personality beyond death. They all go to towards providing a tentative but comprehensive theory/hypothesis rooted in the evidence provided. That evidence is wide-ranging and important, drawn from cases both historical and modern, spontaneous and/or experimental (since both rely on observation), and quite often from the author's considerable personal experience as a researcher. It can also be highly entertaining: my own favourite is where, in a formal experiment with the famous psychic Matthew Manning, the author inadvertently irritates him into producing a positive result.

One might describe this book as a tapestry of micro- and macro- psi phenomena, intertwined with large and small challenges to accepted wisdoms that inspire you to think again and again. When you step back the picture may appear not quite complete (after all, we are only offered a "small theory" and which of us has the big one?), but it is woven together with a self-deprecating dry humour that makes the experience of examining it closely a real pleasure.

Zofie Weaver, December 2018

PREFACE

~

This collection of writings on psychical research cannot be said to cover more than a sample of the field; currently the Psi Encyclopedia on the SPR website contains more than 100 articles, and there are more to come. The collection presented here is based on talks I have given over some twenty years at conferences and lectures on topics that have come to my notice and provoked a response or which raise fundamental questions about the nature of reality and on which I think psychical research findings shed light. Originally addressed to members of the Society for Psychical Research (SPR), the text has been modified in places so as to eliminate specialist language or explain terms that may not be familiar to the general reader, and to be less confrontational in areas where some SPR members may hold opinions that differ from mine.

There have also been modifications to limit repetition of material that figured in more than one talk, with some cross references given here that would have been ineffective when a talk may have been separated by years from another one where the same material was relevant in different contexts. Most of us have some case reports so burnt into the brain that one word or name will bring its details immediately to mind, but to others it may be one of the myriads of case reports buried somewhere in the depths of the memory that can be retrieved only by reminder. Researchers usually have aspects of the subject that they favour and case material that has struck them as highly significant; these may then get quoted as the researcher moves from one theme to another; others may view as a bee in the bonnet material which to that researcher is the key to enlightenment.

Despite a very partial coverage of a vast domain, the shorter conference items of part one are fairly representative of the field in that the first two deal with psycho-physical effects, where tangible incidents occur (such as those that erupt in the course of poltergeist outbreaks), effects that can be seen and heard by those present at the scene; the last two are on the less controversial subjective phenomena of the mind, where people (some psychically endowed on a regular basis and others just taken by surprise) become aware of something they had no normal means of knowing. These phenomena entail no apparent physical manifestations, and seem comfortingly analogous with radio transmission and radar search. The third talk straddles both seemingly separate zones, suggesting that mental and physical effects are not so much distinct aspects of psychic activity but more like two sides of one coin or the inside and outside of a fabric.

Like all complex areas of study, psychical research has its jargon, serving as shorthand for regular users and annoyance for those not familiar with the terms. I don't think that poltergeist activity needs defining, and it takes so many forms that definition would be problematical. To some extent ESP (extra-sensory perception) has entered the language, and it is a convenient term for referring to telepathy and clairvoyance, though these two faculties are, in fact, very different in their modes of operation. They are bracketed together because, at the receiving end of the action, the result is that someone, the telepath or clairvoyant, becomes the recipient of data that he had no way of accessing through the normal channels of sight, sound and touch.

Telepathy is also a term well known to the public, but it is not always made clear that what it covers is awareness of more than one sort of stimulus that originates in the mind of another person, data that might be thoughts, emotions, sensations, experiences (especially crises), and the like. It is not just a matter of information transfer. Telepathy is often described as mind-to- mind transmission, though it seems more like rapport or mental content sharing. However it is conceptualised, it is distinguishable from clairvoyance, in which the clairvoyant becomes aware of facts, incidents, sights, sounds and observable data remote from his perception, but without the assistance of a telepathic source, i.e. a person from whose mind the data is derived, referred to by researchers as the agent, whether that person is taking part volitionally in an experiment or acting involuntarily as a telepathic source.

Other forms of ESP that have been widely studied are precognition and retrocognition. As the name suggests, precognition means foreknowledge of the future, unrelated to extrapolation from present circumstances. None of the articles here deals with precognition, and I would not want to express any definite views on its prevalence. Retrocognition is another matter, and I have had a lot to say. In a way it is the mirror image of precognition, being awareness of the past, but whereas the strongest precognition cases generally refer to the experient's own future, the awareness of one's own past is the function of memory, which though mysterious in its own way is not paranormal; retrocognition is awareness of past events outside one's own experience or knowledge. In the item on 'Telepathy and Clairvoyance' I argue that clairvoyance operates by retrocognition.

After this sampling of physical PK (psychokineses) and mental ESP (extra-sensory perception), the two fundamental aspects of psi[1] (the insider word for the paranormal in all its forms), we pass on to the longer discourses, culminating in what I fancy to be a full exposition of the relationship between the familiar causal world, ever more prodigiously explored and increasingly controlled by science, and the non-causal, therefore uncontrollable, realms of psi.

The first of these more extensive articles focuses on the vital topic not so far mentioned: the strength of the evidence in support of continued existence of individual personalities after death, evidence that can invariably be interpreted in terms of psi operating through living minds. In all cases the question arises as to whether the survival interpretation is more convincing than the living-mind alternatives. In this talk, three cases are discussed, which seem extremely tortuous to explain without invoking some initiative or linkage with the mind of the dead person who is seemingly taking a leading part in the conversation.

This is followed by a look at the sort of research that was being pursued (between the two world wars) in some other countries, especially in France, where French members of their Institut Métapsychique Internatonal (IMI), while respecting their English counterparts and maintaining cordial mutual relations, felt, with some embarrassment, that the English preoccupation with survival was a weakness, a failure to let hold of religion, due (they speculated) to the brainwashing effects

---

[1] Psi (the p being silent in its English usage) is the initial letter of the Greek word transcribed as Psyche, the soul or mind. The more familiar alternative to psi, 'the paranormal', has become somewhat debased by association with implausible ghosts, tall stories and popular entertainment, while more neutral 'psi' should be understood to refer to phenomena that are thought to be reasonably well researched and authenticated.

of attending chapel every day at boarding schools! The IMI, scientists to a man, saw psi as an intriguing branch of biology, exciting for their colleagues but not transformational for mankind in general, this being the aspirational goal of the SPR leaders, which had always included interested members of the public in its membership and whose active researchers were philosophers and classical scholars as well as scientists, and included women both as members and researchers.

The next talk takes up themes from Part One, setting out some more general principles. Having by now had laid out a fair sample of research findings, it deals with the dismissive accusation so often trumpeted, that there is no proof that psi exists at all and that, if challenged, researchers are unable to lay on a demonstration. Another familiar slight is that the so-called evidence for psi consists of anecdotes. One has to admit that this disdainful term is also sometimes applied to spontaneous case reports by those psi researchers who are mainly focused on experimental procedures. It can be retorted that a report of an experimental result that cannot be verified by repetition could also be called anecdotal, which is indeed the view taken by psi-deniers who are no more impressed by experimental results than by reports of incidents. In this talk I stress that in law courts eyewitness testimony is considered the most compelling form of evidence, especially when there are multiple witnesses, and scientists also have to accept the testimony of other specialists, unless they happen to have the same apparatus (a large Hadron collider?) and the same expertise. Knowledge, fact and truth ultimately are determined by what people aver.

Later talks, even when starting from a close-up examination of a particular theme, broaden out to cover the wider field. The cautiously ambitious 'Small theory of everything' (the caution lies in the 'small') does indeed spill out beyond the usual confines of psi theorising, and 'everything' comes with a few pinches of salt. It was actually put together many years ago, and has undergone little in the way of revision; in other words, I still think it stands up, combining logical deduction with something in the nature of personal mythology. It is offered up as suggestive rather than definitive.

Preceding the small theory, and contributing significantly to its tenets, comes an article on the subject of Jott, a class of psycho-physical phenomena that have been noted under various heads from time to time, but not until recently been brought under one single head. This concerns things known to have been placed in a definite location ceasing to be found there, and later being found either in another place or back in the place from which they originated, or never seen again. These annoyances (jott is based on just one of those things) are very readily, and often justifiably, attributed to absent-mind, malobservation, defective memory and other mental vagaries, but in some carefully monitored cases these explanations can be ruled out of reasonable possibility. Rather than retain a considerable degree of repetition, four shorter talks on jott have been removed in favour of one recast piece summarising a variety of cases covering the data, and further considering one of the theoretical issues, namely, the implications of the apparent overriding of causality by incidents of spatial discontinuity, this being the more scientific description of the less alarming jott. Other aspects of jott theory are considered in the wider context of the following chapter.

This more recent talk on Psychic Force was originally given under the less friendly Greek-derived title 'Psychoboulia,' a word that (to borrow a phrase often heard on television news) some people may find upsetting. It means mind exerting its will, and the word has been consigned to history for understandable lack of support. Apart from disconcerting words, the idea of mind controlling matter and determining what we see and experience, may also be disquieting and resistible, but it is an assumption built into several of the previous talks, more especially 'Making things happen' in which it is suggested that unconscious minds, under instructions delivered by telepathic command from a cosmic control, actualise a causal environment. 'Psychic Force' elaborates on that theme, and goes back one stage further, to speculate on the nature and origin of the matter over which mind exerts its influence.

That is the deeper end where we dive into cavernous waters. We start at the safer end, where there are steps-down and a more cautious approach to total immersion.

PART ONE:

FIRST PRINCIPLES

INTRODUCTION

~

There was an interval of twelve years between these two talks (2004 and 2016) so some ideas surfaced in the later talk that were broached in the earlier one, which started by questioning the goals of psychical research. The later talk started with an assertion, one which had built into it anticipation of a certain degree of opposition. Both deal with the problem that lies at the heart of much resistance to acceptance of psi, viz., the 'failure' to deliver scientific proof, whether of ESP at one end of the scale or PK at the other. No one can say that on Wednesday at midday we shall show you someone receiving a veridical telepathic impression that someone dear to her has suffered a crisis, or that a troubled family will be afflicted by a poltergeist. An even greater reproach is that no one can arrange a demonstration of one single target / response test that is certain to yield a result well above chance expectation. These shortcomings are seen as proof that psi is not real.

That this attitude is misconceived is a theme that recurs throughout these articles, and it is dealt with on a broader front in the more substantial talk on proof, but these two shorter items focus especially on the fallacy of treating psi as if it were a branch of physics to be explained and controlled, rather than as comprising a range of real but (in the usual sense) non-causal effects outside the reach of scientific methodology because they are outside sequential causality.

Looking back, twelve years later, at this earlier talk, I can see that expostulation at the wrong-headedness of making explanation and control of psi a principal aim of the society has become a leitmotiv in my approach to psychical research, and these themes will recur. I don't know if this calls for apology or amounts to a recognition that if you want an idea to sink in and take hold you have to air it more than once.

WHAT IS THE POINT OF
PSYCHICAL RESEARCH?

~

W hat, I ask, is the point of psychical research. Does it have agreed aims? And are those aims realisable? What amounts to progress? How do we tell whether we have failed or succeeded? Do we have an end goal, and, if so, what is it? And what do we say, on the one hand to indifferent outsiders, and, on the other hand, to disaffected colleagues and supporters who complain that in more than a century we have not got anywhere, and we are not getting anywhere? Where is that anywhere to which they think we should get?

What started me on this inquiry was finding that for some people we do indeed have an end goal, which is understanding and explaining how and why paranormal effects occur; and, bearing in mind that understanding and explanation usually lead to control, control appears to be the ultimate goal. If that is so, we are certainly not getting anywhere, are probably doomed to failure, and are in a state of regress rather than progress. All very bad news if explanation is truly a realistic and realisable aim and our measure of success. But I should like to enter a note of dissent.

First of all, I draw attention to the words inscribed in the SPR Journal, describing the proposed activities of the society. The founders set out to examine the phenomena now generally known as paranormal – psi in insider language. They saw their remit as investigating and reporting on their findings; this necessarily involved setting out their observations in an orderly manner, so taxonomy and classification are included in the task. One can reasonably say that theorising on the findings is a natural outcome of the examination, but two large words are missing from that statement of purpose – explain and control – the most ambitious of these being control. Explanation, then, let alone control, is not stated to be a primary objective. Nevertheless it remains a discomforting presence, and I should like to see it lifted off our collective shoulders. So let us cast a cold light on explanation, which comes in three main forms.

A. First, there is a straightforward explanation in terms of normal causality and current science; in other words, explaining away an effect that was, at first light, thought to be paranormal. Psi-deniers are, of course, pleased and vindicated when some promising item gets struck off the paranormal menu – and not only psi-deniers. I have known members of the SPR whose instincts are so grounded in the gut feeling that there must be a natural explanation for everything that the elimination, here and there, of a discredited item is seemingly greeted with a rush of endorphins at the restoration of normality to its primacy. It also saves one the trouble of having to pay the matter some attention, when attention is in short supply and the claims on it are huge, from the viewpoint of psi alone. But this sort of triage is not the point of psychical research, any more than weeding is the point of gardening; it is just a necessary chore.

B. At the other end of the scale there are explanations that depend on speculative theories, by which I mean ideas ranging from philosophical at the top end to free fantasy at the other. These theories are more or less personal to the proponents, who are, of course, delighted to share their ideas with all of you. There's a lot of these floating around (I plead guilty myself), some more plausible than others. These are theories that are not susceptible to proof or, indeed, to falsification, and, at best, they can be shown to be compatible with a lot of paranormal phenomena; but they don't actually explain anything in a testable way.

C. Moving away from the extreme ends, there are explanations that seek to show that certain paranormal phenomena are compatible with science as we know it, meaning the proponent's interpretation of currently respected theoretical models of science, which tend to be, or at least to seem to the outsider, even weirder than the paranormal. As to this, the non-scientist can only wait in the wings to see if one of these theories turns out to qualify as a partial explanation. I say partial because they seldom seem to take account of macro-phenomena such as materialisation and poltergeist effects, for which there is substantial evidence.

We come to another three-way division, because, as I see it, an explanatory theory can establish credibility in three different ways.

1. The theory could explain how to produce a paranormal effect.

2. It could explain how to predict time, place, conditions and other circumstances under which a psi incident is going to happen or could be made to happen.

3. It could explain exactly, not just vaguely, why neither of these is possible.

How likely is it that an explanation of one sort or another will be forthcoming, and what would the world be like if this were to come about? The most probable would, I think, be an explanation of the third order, explaining exactly why paranormal phenomena, though indisputably real, cannot be produced to order or have their occurrence predicted.

This would be a very important and crucial theory and one that should impinge on the world outlook of every thinking person. However, I doubt whether, in practice, it would have that impact. For one thing, there would be no universal acceptance of the theory in the same way that scientists accept, as I understand it, Heisenberg's principle that the velocity and position of an electron cannot be determined at the same moment. Psi-deniers would regard such a theory as an admission that there were no paranormal phenomena, and, on the other hand, there would be dissenters convinced that the apparently impregnable theory must be faulty and that there must be some way to explain and control the paranormal.

So what about being able to predict the circumstances under which a paranormal effect will take place, an explanation of the second order? Science can't tell the incoming half-way tide to turn round and go out instead of coming in, but it can tell you that in three hours time this is what it is going to do. Plain observation can also tell you this, but science can go further and say why this happens with such unfailing regularity. Without being able to control planetary movements, scientists can predict those movements. Can one realistically imagine being able, in a similar way, to predict an incident of crisis telepathy?

Could you say, there is an old lady about to die in Australia who has never seen her English grandchild; her mother was a medium, her daughter has been known to see apparitions, it is the seventh day of the seventh month, the moon is full, sidereal time is optimal – the child will almost certainly report next morning that she was briefly visited by a strange old woman that night? Or here is a family where the father drinks, the mother is depressive, the son is in prison, the daughter is pregnant, the rent is unpaid, the boiler has broken down; when they find that the football match scheduled to be shown on television has been cancelled there is going to be a poltergeist outbreak in which light bulbs are thrown around and there will be thunderous knocks on the floor. Even now we might say that this is the sort of family where you might expect a poltergeist but can you imagine turning up with your video just in time to catch it?

Here, as with many other areas of the paranormal, there is no useful analogy with the regularities studied by science – or if there is any analogy, it is rather like trying to predict the weather on this day next year. In the realms of normal life, effects whose causes are well defined can be predicted with such a high degree of probability as to amount to virtual certainty, whereas in the realms of the paranormal the ability to predict will always have such a low probability of success as to amount to a virtual nil prospect.

However, predicting the conditions under which an experimental procedure will succeed is a more plausible concept. And, of course, if you can predict when an experiment will be successful then you are on the way to being able to produce that result to order. Success to order does not mean that if you carry out the procedure 100 or 1000 times you will, or may, find that your results are somewhat better than chance expectation – and you may find that you have to do it 10,000 times or more to be sure of that outcome. That is not what is meant by predictable, nor is it what is meant by demonstrate.

Success could be on a modest statistical scale: you might say that you could guarantee that at that time and place, and using percipients of a selected but not unusual class, then on every trial your demonstrators will score above chance level every time. As a convincing demonstration of the paranormal that would not be too much to ask. And if your theory about experimental conditions is strong enough to ensure that under your specified conditions you will always get a better than chance result, you would have an explanatory theory. And assuming that your faculty of prediction was not limited to some very rare conditions, or very unusual participants, you could claim to produce a paranormal effect to order.

The production of psi to order, independently of any predictions about circumstances or conditions, has occurred from time to time, but in demonstrations by extraordinary psychics, persistently and famously by Alexis Didier (Méheust 2005) and Stefan Ossowiecki (Barrington et al 2005), and occasionally by lesser known psychics. But these demonstrations have not changed the world, because people who have not personally encountered the psychics in question find it easier to disbelieve reports on them and treat their death as further reassurance that witnesses to their prowess were unreliable. 'Show me' they say, when it's too late. The exploits of these two exceptional clairvoyants will figure in later articles.

But a practical technique for controlling demonstrations of the paranormal to order by a wide range of moderately gifted citizens – say, as many as are capable of reading music – that could change the world. From the viewpoint of psychical research and its place in public esteem, things would take a very happy turn. Universities would all have their psi faculties with tenured professors, and any reasonably able student would be able to secure a degree in ESP or PK. The Times would carry advertisements from the Ministry of Defence inviting applications from suitably qualified psychics to keep watch on the international scene, block scrutiny from abroad and give warning of hostile thoughts. The paranormal would finally be a respected and very well funded science. That would indeed be progress. No one could say we hadn't got anywhere.

We would actually have transformed a world of regularities into a mixture of Hogwarts academy and virtual reality. Newspaper science journalists would explain the paranormal in terms the layman could understand and apply. Brawling youths would practise their psychic stoning of windows or frighten old ladies by turning off the lights and change countryside TV programmes to gangster movies. People would be queueing to emigrate to another planet.

How would we have arrived at this goal? Would it be because some extraordinary gifted psychic had found a way to pass his techniques to other psychics by teaching them how to operate? Ossowiecki says that an old man called Froebel taught him how to be a clairvoyant, but Froebel started from the base-line that he instantly recognised in Ossowiecki a natural psychic who had so far used his powers only to entertain his friends by displays of PK (moving furniture around to amuse and astonish). Ossowiecki is one of several high calibre psychics who did in fact describe how he set about reading the past (not his own past) or divining the contents of sealed packages, but that hasn't helped to produce other master psychics. Why should we be surprised? Mozart had pupils, but they did not turn into great composers.

Control is always the point and the aim of science, so, if we arrived at the point of control, or even partial control, over the paranormal it would surely be through the route of science, meaning, inevitably, a greatly expanded science, whether based on quantum mechanisms, strings, implicate orders or something entirely beyond current thinking. If it comes to an expanded science it seems more likely that some of the physical aspects of the paranormal will prove to be related to physics as understood by physicists, and that is an exciting prospect. Indeed the slotting of the whole of the paranormal into super-science is, I think, the Mecca that some of our colleagues feel to be the only destination that could satisfy their hopes and justify their striving.

It is a noble aim, though I have to say that I don't feel at all confident that it's going to happen. I realise that I am articulating the viewpoint of an Edwardian who, a mere 100 years ago, could not imagine airflight and television, let alone nanotechnology and the internet. In another fifty years the world may indeed be unrecognisable. But extrapolating to a physics that embraces the paranormal, assumes that there is a slot within the scientific model into which the paranormal can be fitted. That, I suggest, is not necessarily so. The paranormal, when it erupts, seems to ride roughshod over the regularities of science, which makes it, to my mind, far more likely that our ordered existence fits into a slot of the paranormal reality, a reality that is usually inaccessible to us. If this is so, then the quart is never going to fit into the pint pot, and, to continue the metaphor, it's no use crying over spilt milk. The paranormal exists and therefore fits into something, which one may as well call the greater science, but, if the paranormal is less graspable than the normal, and the normal is mind-bogglingly complex, how way out must be the greater science that encompasses the paranormal.

An aspect of psychical research that has, so far, been left out of consideration is the survival of personal consciousness after death. Even if one can imagine explanations or partial explanations of paranormal cognition and anomalous physical effects, the question would still remain as to how we should interpret phenomena such as phantom materialisation, ostensible communication from the dead, or apparent reincarnation or other cases where living people seem to be influenced by people from a past time. That question will surely always remain open to individual assessment, and it is difficult to see how interpretation of the data could ever be the subject of determination by a scientific theory. When one takes into account the whole picture – the relevance of the paranormal to consciousness, identity, survival, the persistence of the past and foreknowledge of the future – a comprehensive explanatory theory is rather like explaining the purpose of the universe and the meaning of life on earth. I suppose we should all like to know that, but it is, in fact, an ideal rather than a realistic objective, because, while we are all free to speculate about these imponderables, it may be categorically impossible for anyone to advance a provable theory that would amount to a comprehensive explanation. This limitation is surely to be expected and accepted.

There are aims worth pursuing that are, in my view, more realistic and, therefore, more valuable, and nothing strikes me as more important than attempts to reduce segments of our vast and disorderly accumulation of material to order and meaning. It is a fine thing to produce bricks, but, when you have more bricks than the brickyard can accommodate, what really matters is to use them to create meaningful structures. With enough structures you begin to see the outline of possible conclusions, even theories. My idea of failure is not the absence of theory, but the failure to make good use of the goldmines locked up in the vast literature of the past.

Viewed as a science, psychical research can be seen blundering around lamenting its lack of explanatory theories; but viewed as historical ontology, a chronicle of non-conforming facts, it is a treasure of accumulated experience. History has no end goal, so there is no question of history failing. Like history, the chronicles of psychical research record things that happen, whether naturally or by inducement, things that signal a dimension of reality that has the widest possible implications for humankind. The careful examination of those things that have accumulated for our benefit, and continue to accumulate, give us grounds for realising that ordinary things are not quite as they seem to be, and provide reliable material enabling us to speculate rationally and imagine other sorts of reality based on hard evidence. And, in so far as anything in this unsatisfactory world has a point, that, as I see it, is the point of psychical research.

REPEATABLE PSI EXPERIMENT – A CONTRADICTION IN TERMS

~

Psychical research could be defined as the study of unpredictable events and uncontrollable effects. And why is that a defensible proposition? It is because psi means effects without an apparent cause; and if after diligent search a cause appears, the event is not psi. That is how we tell psi from not psi. There are, of course effects within the domain of scientific inquiry where the cause has not been ascertained but is ascertainable; and when ascertained it will be valid for any competent person putting the explanation to the test or making a prediction about the circumstances in which the event will occur. And so it will unless, of course, psi puts a deviant spoke in the causal wheel.

So, the defining essence of a psi effect is that it is not preceded by what is commonly understood as 'a cause' In the context of this talk, causality means a sequential chain of observable events such that each event apparently follows on from the preceding event. Causal events are related only to preceding events in the sequence, and are not related to anyone's beliefs, hopes, moods or other subjective attitudes. Causality is the driver of Newtonian clockwork. So, to make the position clear beyond peradventure, when it comes to a psi incident no cause will be found because there is none to find. And if a psi effect is indeed one without a cause, how can we reliably, repeatably, cause it to happen? The answer has to be that we can't, because if we can cause it, it is not psi.

At this juncture I could, having made the point more than once, and with irrefutable logic, draw a line and print The end. But, there is always room to probe and explore the irrefutably obvious. So we shall explore, starting with the concessionary observation that psi does appear to be in a not-quite-causal relationship with people's desires, needs, fears and expectations, in that a psi-incident often seems to be precipitated by someone's emotional state. This is not clockwork causation as I have defined it, though I also concede that if the emotional psi-trigger could be identified and brought under some useful degree of control, then we might get something approaching a repeatable effect.

It is a big 'if.' Could we ever have a reliable protocol for triggering psi, a protocol that could be utilised by some researchers (if not all) who have some aptitude but are not too exceptional, working with subjects also modestly endowed. The essential feature of a repeatable demonstration in response to a protocolled procedure is that it must not require unusually gifted demonstrators. For, in the judgment of the psi-resistant pundit, exceptionally gifted performers may/must be fraudulent and convinced observers must have been fooled (even if they are very clever in other situations). In any case, stars come and go, and, when they are gone, so are their repeated demonstrations.

Moving on, I readily concede that no procedure involving humans could reasonably be expected to function with the reliability of a chemical reaction; reason requires only that psi could be produced sufficiently to order as to make it readily demonstrable to people willing to be shown but who do not have the patience or the inclination to undertake or sit through a few thousand trials followed up by sophisticated statistics. A reasonable requirement is that a fair range of researcher/psychic teams would be able to demonstrate psi effects with the same reliability as a fair range of hynotist/hypnotee teams demonstrating hypnosis.

But, though in past times there was a strong link between hypnosis/ mesmerism and the emergence of clairvoyance, the association is no longer demonstrable. There is now a large difference between hypnotic induction and unrelated attempts to elicit psi to order; a hypnotist may not know exactly why and how his techniques are working, but he is choosing the words he is speaking, the gestures he is making, the articles he is using. He knows what usually works for him and he is able to demonstrate his control over the hypnotee, because he knows what he is doing. The psychical researcher hasn't the least idea how to induce someone to turn a light on and off remotely or describe the contents of a sealed container or transmit a telepathic impression or receive one, and no more has the would-be psychic any idea how to accomplish these things. Those who can, do, in the same way that they can raise an arm, without knowing how or why it is accomplished. The difference is that most people can will their arm to rise, but they can't do the same to a table by holding their hands over it.

If pressed for how to produce psi, the psychic might say something like 'I put myself into a state where there is no boundary between me and the rest of creation' but he cannot say how to bring this state about. Mediums such as Leonore Piper[2] had to be in a trance to function, and Alexis Didier, whose remarkable clairvoyance will be the subject of articles in Part Two, had to be hypnotized before he could perform, but the hypnotic induction did not include directions about how to demonstrate psi. They not only didn't know what they were doing, they didn't even know what they had done. It was all done by that invisible servant in the unconscious: the one who brings you words and names you have forgotten and answers to crossword clues; the one who acts like a cross between Figaro, Jeeves and Sir Humphrey Appleby, and, like them, does things his own way.

So, if a functioning psychic does not know what he is doing, and can't give useful directions to someone else, how on earth is an average citizen – even one selected for some degree of aptitude – supposed to perform to order? It is true that when it comes to experimentation using the average citizen, or more usually the average psychology student, as subjects, it is widely thought to be the experimenter who jollies them into better than chance demonstrations, whether through belief and confidence in the protocol he has devised or by personal charisma. But, as to how to release the psi faculty, he has no more idea than the subjects he is trying to enthuse.

The crucial question is whether or not this is due to ignorance that could be remedied by systematic inquiry. Medical research can advance treatment by increasing understanding of biological processes; could greater understanding of physical and psychological processes lead to greater control? Or is it in the nature of things that the mechanisms of psi are outside conscious control just as the circulation of the blood operates outside conscious control. I believe some individuals claim to exercise a degree of control over circulation, rather as some psi virtuosi can demonstrate a degree of control over psi, but a general inability does seem to be the state of play so far as the typical human is concerned, the sort who might have one or two psi experiences in

[2] Renowned early twentieth century American mental medium who cooperated over many years with researchers.

a lifetime, but who never knowingly produces a psi effect – in other words, the sort of person whom followers of the Rhine school[3] want to be able to demonstrate psi.

Whether we look at entranced mediums, naturally occurring incidents or experimental procedures, all the indications are that psi operates outside conscious control; let's look at a few examples that reinforce the point.

In the field of spontaneous reports, my favourite, which I have cited before, comes from Dr Louisa Rhine (Rhine 1981), the under-celebrated wife of J B Rhine. She thought that there was little to be learnt from the sort of 'anecdote' that she was reporting, and she reserved her respect for experimental work. I would say that she was undervaluing her contribution. In one of those rare incidents taken from her own experience you can learn a lot. I think it is worth citing again (and again).

Her five-year-old daughter, Betty, was playing on the floor, while Louisa was drinking a cup of coffee and wondering whether to have a biscuit with it. Betty was grizzling that her mother never took her to the theatre. Louisa decided against the biscuit, because, she said to herself, she was getting fat (though a photograph shows that she was not what other people would call fat). As soon as this 'fat' thought had flashed through her mind Betty, without ceasing her play on the floor, piped up and said 'Yes, you've never been fatter.' Duly astounded, Louisa asked Betty why she had said that, and Betty, carrying on with her own agenda about the theatre, said 'Because you never do take me.'

I find this revelatory in several ways: one, that someone receiving data telepathically may have no conscious awareness of receiving it, or of reacting to it, and may even respond in relevant words without knowing she had spoken. Another is that the telepathic emitter can externalise a thought without having the slightest desire to do so, a thought that she might prefer to keep private, and the thought may be picked up by someone without the remotest interest in receiving it – all this without the slightest hint of intentional input from anyone.

In most reports it seems that the unconscious faculty does take its cue from the conscious needs of the telepathic emitter, though often

---

[3]   In the 1930s Prof. J.B. Rhine, of Duke University, USA, argued that academics should advance parapsychology by avoiding virtuoso psychics and work, instead, with groups of ordinary people, whose minimal psi ability would be shown to accumulate to statistical significance. Ever since then university research has been on these lines.

not always in a way that is a literal reflection of conscious thoughts. Another case I have cited before is taken from Dr Ian Stevenson's paper on telepathic impressions. (Stevenson 1970) A married couple got into trouble with their pleasure boat and were shipwrecked in a place from which rescue seemed ever more unlikely as days went by and death seemed close at hand. There had been a prolonged rift between them and their son and his wife, and they felt acute sorrow at the thought of perishing with the rift unhealed. At the receiving end, the daughter-in-law, the pivotal character in the rift, had a recurrent waking vision of her parents-in-law looking at her with hands outstretched in gestures of supplication. Finally she told her husband, who made inquiries, arranged a search and secured a last minute rescue, and the rift was healed. But the very effective vision seen by the daughter-in-law did not correspond with any action taken or imagined by the parents. The unconscious goes about its business in its own way. In this case it laid on a performance that the afflicted parents would hardly have enacted themselves and which they might have regarded with some embarrassment.

In another of Stevenson's impression cases a woman he called Dora was suddenly afflicted with severe pain. Fortunately for her, and even more so for us, her husband was a physician, and, while she moaned and thrashed around for several hours, he could find absolutely nothing wrong with her. It turned out that at that time her twin sister Martha was unexpectedly giving birth, and having such a terrible time that she had lapsed into a coma at the time when Dora was suffering birth pangs. You don't get much more unconscious than that.

These illustrations are taken from real life situations, but experimental research tells the same story. In fact, it gives so many indications that psi operates via the unconscious, I am surprised that anyone ever asks for a conscious response. In a case from the 1920s, involving no technology, the Polish medium Olga Kahl was celebrated for responding to targets such as diagrams by displaying them in red outline on her skin, usually without her having any conscious awareness of what it was that was being displayed.

In recent times, one of the clearest examples I have ever seen was shown in a not very distinguished television programme. Two rather down to earth identical twin youths were asked if they had ever experienced telepathic rapport and robustly asserted that they never had. They were then separated and wired up to monitor their physiological responses. After a little time one twin was suddenly given an electric shock, to which he reacted vigorously, while the other one, shown on a split screen, registered nothing at all. However, when the charts were examined the chart of the unscathed twin showed exactly the same peaking of the recording needle as the peak shown on the chart of the twin who had received the shock. But all this drama took place below the threshold of consciousness.

Of course, being popular television this would have been at best re-enacted and at worst invented, but the late Guy Lyon Playfair[4] assured me that he has seen the same effect under test conditions (Playfair 2015), and I quote the TV performance because I saw it, and also bearing in mind that TV usually rejoices in putting down psi rather than supporting its reality. I suspect that there may be more people like the youth, whose consciousness was unruffled by the shock to his autonomic system, than there are like very aware twin Martha, whose conscious mind was presumably more in touch with convulsions in the unconscious.

Can the normal citizen learn anything from the psi virtuoso? I rather doubt it. In some activities there seems to be a continuum between the virtuoso performer and the average person. If you ignore market value, there seem to be a lot of little known artists and even amateurs who can produce a superb painting or drawing but you are less likely to encounter a superb string quartet knocked up by a musically inclined retired civil servant. I would think that for psi endowment there is a sharp division, even sharper than in musical endowment, and, when asked to exercise psi consciously, the man in the street probably never gets beyond the psi equivalent of "Chopsticks".

More than natural endowment, I would think that the star psychic is, in a benign way, abnormal, rather like a high functioning autistic person with a genius for hacking computers, and when I say 'benign' I mean that I am not aware of any balancing personality deficits in psychics equivalent to the sort of social penalty that autistic geniuses seem to suffer as quid pro quo for their extraordinary powers. But I should still characterise the star psychic's Factor X as an abnormality. And I fall in with the pronouncement of the magician, Jean-Eugène Robert-Houdin, who said that he could teach Alexis Didier the arts of conjuring, but he could not learn from Alexis how to practise the arts of the clairvoyant. Like nearly all of us, he did not have Factor X.

---

[4] Colleague and distinguished author of books dealing with psi, including *Twin Telepathy*

(More to come about this encounter between the master psychic and the master magician in the talk on dishonest disbelief).

The factor X people seem to have a porous membrane that permits a high degree of interchange between conscious and unconscious, psi-emitters (whose output is telepathic transmission) passing their motivations down to the unconscious for externalisation, and psi-receivers (whose input is ESP) dredging up material that probably seethes around in the subconscious of normal people but never rises to the surface.

Apart from this factor X, it is difficult to see what else unites the virtuoso psychic performers: farm boy Indridi Indridison, probably the most sensational physical and mental medium of all time, (Haraldsson et al. 2015); banker and journalist Kluski (Weaver 2015), not far behind Indridi on both fronts; actor Alexis Didier, engineer Stefan Ossowiecki, classical scholar, Margaret Verrall, and housewife, Leonore Piper (both remarkable mental late nineteenth and early twentieth-century mediums), to mention a few star psychics who seem widely disparate in character, temperament, social position and education. What seems pretty clear is that factor X is not part of the normal human condition, which is to have a fairly resistant filter between the conscious mind and the unconscious depths where control over psi is evidently located.

There is probably a good reason for this filter. It may be because the unconscious is, as I have suggested elsewhere, largely engaged in maintaining the causal environment around us, telepathically receiving instructions from the universal control mechanism and exercising powers of PK to put its codes into effect. (These ideas are put forward and developed in the final article on psychic force). Consistently with that, we see that when the psi virtuoso accesses those unconscious regions and interferes with their routine duties, environmental consistency in that location fails and chaos breaks out in seance rooms. But before long causal order asserts itself, disturbances peter out, normal life is restored, and so are the filters. It looks as if the filters are there to protect us from mental confusion and sequential reality breakdown.

The science fiction writer Arthur C. Clarke wrote a novel (Childhood's End) about how a new generation of children becomes telepathic – I think it was something to do with a mutation and a bit of interference from cosmic visitors – and their parents look on aghast at an alien tribe of hyper-facebookers constantly consulting their telepathic hyperphones. I don't think any of us are expecting a worldwide mutation, but there do seem to be hopes that some higher degree of mindfulness could lead to some degree of mastery over psi. It would be an unusual route because the natural master psychics don't seem to have put any effort into acquiring their gift, and still less does the poltergeist focus person, reluctant virtuoso on whom the X factor is imposed for a limited time.

And we would be back to the exceptional person, because as far as the rest of us are concerned, I doubt whether the unconscious powers of psi ever have been or will be or should be readily accessible to conscious control. It is one thing for an occasional shock wave to send out a warning or message and for an interested party to receive it (I am talking mainly about cases of crisis telepathy, where any one of us, perhaps once in a lifetime, may become aware of some distant disaster befalling someone closely linked to us) but frequent intrusions into the mind would send us into a state of mental and emotional turmoil. We seem to have evolved to keep our conscious minds to ourselves, and I don't see anything changing that, short of some rather radical and improbable genetic engineering.

I can see that this may look like bad news, in that control of repeatable experiments would engage the interest of some currently indifferent scientists; but I think that prospect is doomed, and, if we allow the reality and importance of psi to be determined by the production of a protocol for the ready demonstration of psi, we shall always be judged to have failed in a supreme aim, an acid test foisted on psychical researchers by outsiders who have no concept of psi and its implications. The manifestations of psi tell us that the causal world of common experience is not the only reality, a message that seems also to be suggested in rather similar terms by some concepts in physics, and it would be very fruitful if we could engage the interest of physicists open to the essential and elusive nature of psi.

So, in short, let us make it clear to the world that psychical research is not about protocols for repeatable experiments. It is not in the nature of the beast to respond to attempts at control. You should not try to get cats to herd sheep. Your efforts will result in failure, because it is not what they do. They, like psychical research, have other qualities to be celebrated.

PART TWO:

SUNDRY TOPICS IN BRIEF

INTRODUCTION

~

T hough the next group of short articles appears under the heading of 'sundry' the first three have a common thread running through them, namely, that people in general may have greater powers than they know they have (or can control) to bend the course of events in the direction that serves their purposes. These influences might be manifest in the environment, as when stones or other articles are hurled or manipulated, or they might influence the ideas in other people's minds (arguably, by the same psychokinetic force) but acting on a subtler scale on another person's mind, whether directly by mind to mind fusion or by modifying the other person's brain content.

The theme of active endeavour (as opposed to passive reception) continues in the article differentiating the activity of clairvoyant perception from the passive action of receiving and becoming aware of telepathic material from an agent. The unusual proposal here is that whereas telepathic connections are made in contemporary time (perhaps in the ever-elusive present moment), clairvoyance is effected by an active search for the target material in the past (whether some time last year or just now and continuing), i.e. by retrocognition. This contention calls for justification, and supporting arguments are put forward.

Unlike telepathic receivers, dependent on spontaneous telepathic emission from an agent, virtuoso clairvoyants, sole practitioners, have been able to give clear and instantaneous demonstrations of clairvoyance. Alexis Didier willingly agreed to a request by an aristocratic Spiritualist to expose his powers to the scrutiny of the most illustrious magician of the day, Jean-Eugène Robert-Houdin. After the demonstration the magician, to his great surprise, had to agree with the aristocrat's published announcement that Didier's clairvoyance was genuine, and beyond any powers of a magician to explain or reproduce. How this was reported by a biographer of Houdin, who could not bear to admit that his hero was convinced (or deceived) by a clairvoyant, is displayed in all its effrontery.

CAN HATRED THROW STONES?

~

There is a rather quirky poem by Robert Browning called the Soliloquy of the Spanish Cloister, in which a monk expresses some very un-brotherly feelings about one of his brethren. I quote:

> There goes my heart's abhorrence,
> Water your damned flowerpots, do;
> If hate killed men, Brother Lawrence,
> God's blood, would not mine kill you.

As brother Lawrence continued to water his flowerpots, it seems that hate did not kill him. But if Browning had shared his wife Elizabeth Barrett Browning's interest in psychical research he might have encompassed the occurrence of something rather nasty in Brother Lawrence's potting shed. Something very nasty went on for many years in a south London suburb where poltergeist manifestations of every sort made life extremely upsetting for Carol Finn (pseudonym) – an intelligent and down to earth woman in a responsible job – and her mother and her younger brother. In its early stages these disturbances, which started outside the house, were reported in the local press, but here pseudonyms are, of course, used for the whole family.

The manifestations in this case, which were on a very large scale, started in 1986, nearly ten years after the family had lived happily in the house untroubled, but fairly soon after Carol's nephew, Gary, moved in, at the age of nineteen. By the time SPR members got to know about it, Carol Finn's house had been subjected to almost daily stoning for more than three years and all the windows were covered with chicken wire to protect them from the large stones that struck the exterior on most days and nights. I saw a large file of correspondence between Carol and the local police, who were severely castigated by her for their failure to catch the presumed vandals.

But when Maurice Grosse, one of the first SPR investigators on the scene, suggested to a sturdily reluctant Carol (What? Ghosts? Nonsense!) that paranormal activity might be responsible, then the stone-throwing became intermittent and violent phenomena started to take place inside the house.

One reason that a lengthy paper has not been submitted to the SPR Journal on this case is that nothing would ever happen when investigators were present. I was frequently there to witness scenes of devastation: a flood that had no ascertainable cause, glass embedded in the wall from bottles of milk flung across the room, an upturned pot of paint in the refrigerator, and so on. But every resident could be exonerated from several of the main incidents, and I see no room to doubt that the phenomena were paranormal. If (as I suspect) the primary motivation behind the poltergeistery was to make the house look very unattractive outside and uncomfortable inside, that object was well and truly achieved, with its conservatory boarded up and front door daubed from time to time.

The dramatis personae are very important in this case, so I shall describe them. Carol was in her mid forties when the activities began. As I have indicated, she had and has a totally outgoing, frank and friendly personality, radiating common sense, responsibility and self-confidence, with good sense of humour, seemingly devoid, so far as is humanly possible, of hang-ups. She had, living with her, her mother and brother and a lot of household pets. Contrary to my expectations, before meeting her, she obviously enjoyed this family life, and was altogether the sort of person who ought not to have had a poltergeist. In fact, she was usually, though not always, at work when things happened.

Her younger brother, Malcolm, was a decorator, very good natured, but lacking Carol's education and intelligence. Whereas she has risen in the social scale and could pass as former head girl of Cheltenham Ladies College, Malcolm has slipped down a notch, but he was kind, polite and tenderly devoted to an extremely old and decrepit dog. Carol was very protective about Malcolm, and greatly resented my initial assumption that he might be knowingly responsible for some of the phenomena. Everyone was, naturally, a suspect initially.

In addition to the dogs, Carol's mother cared for some rescued cats, though these were gone by the time mother died, in the late 1990s, since when there have been no phenomena; but don't imagine that Carol's mother sneaked down in the middle of the night and spent several hours standing on chairs decorating the kitchen ceiling with intricate patterns composed of Branston pickle, because I'm sure she could not and did not. For one thing, at the time of this event she was sharing her bedroom with Carol, and both she and the dogs would have noticed her, or anyone else, going downstairs and beavering away in the middle of the night at a rather noisy, dirty and smelly activity. I am equally sure that she didn't unscrew light bulbs from the chandelier and throw them around.

The reason that Carol and her mother shared a bedroom is that when Carol's nephew Gary was still a teenager Carol took him in to live in her house, and gave up her small front room to him, moving in with her mother. Gary left home because, it seems, his sister had said that either he went or she went, and their mother preferred her daughter. But Gary had been spending most of his time at Carol's house since the age of sixteen, and he was there – but inside the house – when the first stone was thrown. Gary was a rather graceless youth, full of unrealistic ambitions and with a fixation on bodybuilding. Gary is a significant presence in the story, but the main player (mostly off-stage) is his mother, Muriel, for, if hate could kill, Carol would have fallen victim to her younger sister Muriel a long time ago. No less hostile was Muriel's husband, Gary's father.

I knew very little about Muriel until later in the saga, when I caught up with Carol after a long fallow period during which we just exchanged Christmas cards. Since her mother's death Carol had been thinking hard about what lay behind the phenomena, which she had always felt to be a very hostile force directed at her. She told me about an incident that could be a key to the whole action. It goes back to the time when her mother was alive but Gary, by that time, was spending most of his time staying with his girlfriend. But, first of all, here is some back history to shed some light on the hostility of Muriel and her husband to Carol and also to her mother.

In the early 1970s, before the start of mega property-price inflation, Carol decided to put her savings into house purchase, and, as her mother was to live in the house too, mother contributed her small amount of capital. That house was sold at a profit and, in 1976, Carol bought the house where she still lived, in Stonely Grove, as I call it. Muriel had married a builder, but they continued to rent. Muriel expressed some considerable resentment that her mother had 'favoured' Carol by contributing money to her house purchase, and the fact that their mother was also to live there did not, in Muriel's eyes, justify this subsidy to Carol, though at the time it was a relatively small sore point.

But we know what has happened to houses in the London area; over twenty-five years they rocketed in value and become worth about 100 times more than their purchase price, while people who rent have to pay ever more to keep up with the increased freehold values. Muriel's small sore point inflated at about the same rate as the property market, and became a matter of barely contained envy and resentment. The key incident about to be related describes an occasion when the venom was not contained.

Carol had reluctantly complied with her mother's wish to invite Muriel and her husband to lunch. One o'clock came, 2 o'clock, and near to 3 o'clock they arrived, angrily complaining about traffic, though not actually apologising for coming very late indeed. Carol handed out glasses of wine, but found it difficult to make polite conversation. Muriel asked somewhat aggressively what was the matter with her, to which Carol replied that she was rather hungry after the long wait.

Muriel responded by doing two things: first, she threw her glass of wine at Carol, who put up a hand to protect her face; whereupon a shard of glass embedded itself in her hand with such vigour that instead of having lunch she had to be taken to the hospital for stitches. As a mere aside, I consider it strange that the glass should have shattered either in mid-air or on contact with the palm of a hand, and, if it was broken before being thrown, you might have expected Muriel to suffer injury – but let us leave that hanging in the air. It is the words that accompanied the flung wine glass that are really significant. Out of a conversational vacuum Muriel shouted with superb irrelevance: "And you can keep your bloody house!" No one had mentioned the house, least of all Carol, who had said only that she was hungry; so it is likely enough that Muriel and her husband must have been having a smouldering conversation on this subject as they finally drove up to it. The throwing of the wineglass, with sufficient violence to injure Carol, and the bitter words about the house, all point to a festering resentment directed at Carol, but embracing her mother, Malcolm and, incidentally, the dogs, who have also been the victims of thrown objects and even more peculiar things. The Finn poltergeist was definitely more malicious than playful.

Thinking back to the phenomena in the light of this hatred directed at the house and the people who were benefiting from it, one can begin to see things falling into place. As I have said, Gary was there when the first stone was thrown. He was with Malcolm when the stone came hurtling through the kitchen window, and they rushed to peer through the window to see who might be responsible. The only vantage point from which it could reasonably have been projected was their own garden, and there was no one there. I say 'reasonably' because the garden that backed on to theirs would be a considerable distance away from the window.

As it happens, the owner of that garden was standing close to the boundary fence, looking towards Carol's house, and looking very startled. They looked at him and found that he was looking at them. That is a strange thing for the neighbour to do if, for some unknown reason, he had hurled the stone – you would expect him to be pretending to weed the lawn, or something like that – but it is consistent with his seeing a stone flying through the air and wondering where it came from. As it happens, the man died a few weeks later, but the stone-throwing burgeoned.

That the unloved Gary should have moved into Carol's house must surely have been a further irritant for Muriel – a silent reproach that she, his mother, had not wanted him while Carol, merely his aunt, had taken him in, and given him her room, and her TV, and given him the shelter and comfort that he would have expected to get from his own parents. Though, of course, I originally cast graceless Gary as the most likely suspect, he had to be eliminated from many of the incidents. Carol's mother described to me how she, Malcolm and Gary had been peaceably sitting in the living room in full view of one another (Carol was at work) when some milk bottles that had been in the hall were flung from the hall across the room. Carol's mother recalled, with something of a shudder, how excited Gary had been by the display of force. I see Gary not as a perpetrator but as a sort of psychometric object, an aerial or perhaps a tuned circuit, facilitating reception of his mother's malice towards the house and its people. And it was, of course, the house that was the original target, the house that was struck by stones and had its windows broken and made to look a shambles.

It is worth recording that even before the first stone arrived, there was a sort of prelude. Malcolm had painted all the outside window frames and the front door; as soon as he had finished, next day they found that heaps of ripe blackberries had been thrown at the door and the window frames, staining them with unsightly purple blotches.

I am not convinced that this was paranormal. Incredible to relate, Muriel's husband had a rather juvenile and dangerous hobby of projecting objects from a large catapult and may have been the precipitating factor behind the paranormal stoning. I am reminded of an incident in which the physical medium Eusapia Palladino shook her fist at the door on the other side of the room, and a knocking sound was heard on the door as if it had actually been struck by her fist. It could be that in poltergeist cases paranormal action mimics and builds on normal action that a hostile personality sets in motion.

I expect you will wonder if the catapulting husband actually spent more than ten years slinging stones at the house. He lived only about five miles away, but in the early days – and years – police kept watch on the house for hours at a time, and were on duty when stones hit the house, and I don't see how they could have failed to catch him if he did throw or sling stones; but the clinching point is that when Maurice Grosse talked about the resemblance to poltergeist activity, the spook came in from the cold. And Muriel's husband certainly didn't come into the room, where the family members were sitting, and unscrew light bulbs from the chandelier and throw them around.

Initially it seems to have been only Gary who was suffering from the sort of stress one associates with Poltergeist activity, though even the laid-back Carol must have been getting pretty desperate at having her house continually vandalised. But, if we are looking for some other sources of household stress, let's consider Carol's mother. Even if Carol was her preferred daughter, it was disturbing to have another daughter so deeply antagonistic. Moreover it was my impression that she was not entirely pleased at having Gary around, and not at all happy about having him living in the house. She had been fond of him when he was a boy, but boys can become yobbish young men, and, as she made clear to me, she was afraid of his fixation on strength, power and muscle. And it was not only Carol who sacrificed a bedroom of her own – her mother had to share hers with Carol. I don't suppose she liked that at all, but probably felt that it would be selfish and ungrandmotherly to refuse to fall in with Carol's willingness to rough it. I have no doubt that she was highly relieved when, in 1993, Gary finally went off and moved in with his girlfriend. His departure marked a steady decline in manifestations, which ceased altogether with the death of Carol's mother in 1997.

My conclusion is that Muriel's hatred, her husband's catapulting and Gary's love of power displays could have been the constituents of the powerhouse that gave rise to the paranormal action, shaped and sustained it. In some societies, regarded in un-PC terms as backward, a man who falls ill asks 'Who is doing this to me?' the assumption being that someone is sticking pins in his image or burning a hair from his head. I don't see Muriel and her family attempting some Hammer horror technique, because it would never occur to them that it might work, but I can imagine their subconscious getting up to all sorts of horrible things.

It is quite usual, when looking around for a someone who can be regarded as psychically responsible for poltergeist activity, to scrutinise first the inhabitants of the house, especially the adolescents, if any, and then to ask about deceased inhabitants, or anyone else up there who might be trying to attract attention or make trouble. If this theorising about sibling envy and malice is on target, then we should add to questions: Is there anyone out there who hates you, your family, your money, your success or your house?

MAKING THINGS HAPPEN

~

There are two somewhat opposed ways of trying get to grips with psychic phenomena: one is to look at the natural habits of the beast, and the other is to examine its inner workings with a microscope, with a view to scrutinising its cell structure, genetics, and even its atomics and subatomics – though this might have to involve killing it first. We are, of course, talking about the familiar divide between psychical research (ancient art) and parapsychology[5] (modern science), Cavaliers and Roundheads. In so far as these differing approaches may lead to conclusions, theories, hypotheses or mere speculations, they are likely to be unrelated. As in physics itself, top-down does not quite mesh with bottom-up.

In the field of paranormal investigation, the much more respectable and respected Roundheads actually have a harder time. A parapsychologist aims to control and prescribe, good scientific objectives. But all too often, successful procedures carried out by one researcher do not consistently lead to the same results when carried out by others: a sadly unscientific outcome. If Roundheads have theories, they have to be scientific theories, and even if they can't explain or predict, at least their experiments have to work – and work for everyone who follows the directions, not just for one university department or one generation or even one country.

---

5   Some researchers, and most Americans, use the term 'parapsychology' to cover the whole field of psychical research, but I am using it in the more restricted sense of experimentation using psychology based methodology in which groups of mostly unselected subjects, usually students, are used in experiments that have to be assessed for outcome by statistics because the level of correct response is minimal.

Cavaliers don't have these difficulties. If a strikingly paranormal, well-witnessed, fully documented and competently researched event or experimentally induced large-scale effect turns out to be uniquely grotesque, this is not a problem (at least, not a problem to other Cavaliers). It is a colourful addition to a disorderly heap of mosaic pieces, another item to amplify the ever-evolving conglomerate that constitutes the unruly subject matter of psychical research. And if Cavaliers have theories or speculations, they don't actually have to prove themselves by working any more than the theories of Plato or Wittgenstein have to work; they just have to be self-consistent and compatible with well established phenomena, and the measure of cogency is the degree of consistency and compatibility. What follows is that sort of speculation.

It has been noted over the years that extroverts are more paranormal prone than introverts, and, at the extreme ends, you get researchers who can readily be classed as audacious and pioneering, while others take a more cautious approach. At the bold end are some who seem to have a Midas touch, and these are people I call originators. Originators have a strong belief in themselves – not in the sense of egoism or self-glorification, but rather belief in their own creative ideas or belief that under their direction certain things can happen. The originator might prefer to think of this self-belief as intellectual confidence, based on logic and reason, but its emotional impact is more like that of belief. And my thesis, in which I have some degree of confidence (definitely my preferred word) is that originators actually make things happen.

~

Originators are not a separate species of human. If originators make things happen, so does everyone else, to some small degree. It is just that originators do it much more conspicuously. No one open to psychical research findings should find it incredible to posit that people in general are connected by some sort of subconscious telepathic internet, and it seems plausible to take a further step and posit that people who gather together with a common purpose and have an agreed expectation may form a close telepathic network, and that their collective power may be co-ordinated, directed and put to use by the beliefs, purposes and expectations of an originator. To move from the general to the particular, let me cite a few examples where the influence of originators is most striking.

Consider, first, the reports of Dr. W. J. Crawford on his sittings with the Goligher circle in Belfast between 1915 and 1919 (Crawford 1918 and 1919). The Golighers were a simple but respectable Belfast working family who regularly held Spiritualist séances in their attic room, treating these meetings as quasi-religious services. Sixteen-year-old Kathleen was acknowledged to be the medium. Somehow Crawford was invited or permitted to study their activities and carry out a prolonged series of experiments. Not many people will be familiar with his three extraordinary books[6] on psychic structures in the Goligher circle, and perhaps some of those who have read them conclude that Crawford was not only a highly qualified mechanical engineer but also a delusional fantasist. This was also my view until I read an account of Crawford's Goligher circle by Sir William Barrett, a perfectly sane physicist, FRS, founder member and past President of the SPR. He attended one of the sittings, together with his wife, a remarkable woman who, in pre-first world war England, was a physician and hospital director. No fool she, and who can doubt that she and Barrett would have discussed the sitting and compared impressions. Barrett wrote a detailed account that verifies most of the phenomena that Crawford claimed to be able to get the circle to demonstrate, and to demonstrate on request, and immediately on request (Barrett 1918). Later Crawford laid on a similar performance for Whately Carington, a very experienced researcher, who wrote up a very detailed report (Smith 1918) .

The performance included getting a large table, which no one was touching, to rise up and cling to the ceiling so that it could not be pulled down, and to throw anyone off who sat on it, or to pin them against the wall. A so-called trumpet (a cone shaped object, not a musical instrument), would dance around and challenge Barrett or Carington to seize it, but dodge away when they tried. The ectoplasm extruded from Kathleen Goligher (according to Crawford's theoretical model) was asked to make itself into thick pseudopods to bang on the floor and also into delicate little fingers to make sharp raps, and, for a minute or two, a sort of percussion band let loose a tremendous uproar. This circus took place by firelight sufficient to see the location of all the sitters. Kathleen, for reasons that will emerge, was firmly ensconced in a wheelchair that was moored in position on the platform of a weighing machine.

Crawford had control over table movements and other effects to a degree unmatched by any other researcher. Victorian investigators working with physical mediums would make requests to the medium's supposed spirit controller, but they had to take what the spirits gave

---

[6] Crawford 1916, 1919, 1921

them. A generation or two later, scientific researchers like Charles Richet (French Nobel prize-winning physiologist) had no truck with spirits, and made their requests to the medium, getting similarly erratic responses. Crawford addressed himself, with total conviction, to what he called the Operators, whom he believed to be spirit entities who were intelligently co-operating with him like scientific colleagues; and whatever he asked for, that's what he got. Table please rise to a height of eighteen inches and stay there for a few minutes while I make a careful note of the weighing machine readings to check on how much weight has been added to the medium, and now please go six inches higher – and that is what the table did. No one else has been able to manage table movements and other phenomena like that; but no one else has had Operators. Crawford said that he didn't require or expect other people to believe in them, but he did. It seems to have made him an originator par excellence.

Believer as he was in his operators, Crawford remained ever the mechanical engineer, and he reasoned that something material must be supporting the table; this was ectoplasm, a substance produced by Spiritualist mediums, which streamed from the 'trunk' (as he put it) of the medium. Crawford reasoned that when the table rose its weight must be transferred to the weight of the medium, the connected source of the ectoplasm, and that it must form a cantilever to raise the table. It followed that when the table reached a certain critical height it would need support from the floor, so the ectoplasm forming the cantilever would have to drop a perpendicular. When it reached the floor it would press down, so Crawford placed a bell push on the floor, and, obedient to his expectations, the descending extrusion rang the bell. The main focus of Crawford's experimentation was to take readings of the fluctuations in the weight of the medium as the table yo-yo-ed up and down, and dozens of these experiments are recorded in a manner as matter-of-fact as if he were weighing sacks of potatoes. The astonishing thing about Crawford is that despite his reports being beyond the usual boggle threshold of credibility, he never troubled to mention the occasional outside researcher who attended his sittings and could have backed up his account of what took place. It is fortunate that Barrett and Carington wrote independent reports.

The Goligher's gas-lit attic seems to have been a domain apart from the world as we know it. Crawford took a Spiritualist circle centred on communing with spirits and moulded them into a physical phenomena group in which his theories were acted out. Would one expect another group to get cantilevers dropping perpendiculars onto bell pushes? Well, I wouldn't. But it does not mean that it did not happen for its confident originator and his devoted circle.

It is time to mention that other class of researcher, who, in relation to an originator, is an adopter. We know that people who adopt can be as devoted to their adopted charges as birth parents, and, in psychical research, an adopter is one who is so taken with the originator's idea that he feels almost equally positive and protective. An adopter may have his own take on the idea to the extent that he functions as a co-originator, and then you get positive results from a group of the like-minded. But, further down the line, enthusiasm falls off, and so do effects. At the end of the line are the dutiful replicators, who do not share the originator's proprietary drive at all, but think it would be good and useful to follow the prescribed procedure and see if they and their team get the same results. But it is not their baby, they don't love it, and they cannot make it do as it's told. And the hostile replicator, who really wants the baby thrown out, can operate as an anti-originator: end of baby wonder, reported gleefully in the press.

It is not entirely in the field of experimentally induced phenomena that the hand of the originator may seem to be guiding the course of events. In the Paranormal Review of April 2012 I summarised (Barrington 2012) two mind-blowing poltergeist reports from Czechoslovakia (presented by Professsor A. Von Schrenck-Notzing in the Zeitschrift für Parapsychologie of 1928). Hans Wratnik, an Austrian high school schoolteacher, when reporting the first case, was convinced that it was the encounter between the thirteen-year-old Tibor, clearly the poltergeist focus, and his older cousin, Lazy, that powered the manifestations, which were initially stone-throwing, but with the twist that stones also materialised inside houses – and lots more. Wratnik theorised that if he separated Tibor from his cousin, everything would stop, because it would be like unplugging a positive terminal – the younger person – from a negative – the friendly somewhat older person. In Tibor's case this worked like a charm. But, if Wratnik had had any prior acquaintance with poltergeist literature, he would have known that numerous cases have been reported where no such combination was present and he would not have had so much confidence in his electrical analogy.

He must have been agog to hear of another case where his theory could be vindicated, and behold, shortly afterwards, fourteen-year-old Hilda, who actually lived in Wratnik's village, went to stay with the family of her young aunt in a Czech village about twenty miles away, whereupon keys turned by themselves in locks, beans jumped out of bags, things moved from closed rooms and there was general pandemonium. Again, Wratnik could quieten things down by separating Hilda from her aunt, reflecting his belief in the power of the sympathetic bond. But actually in poltergeist cases you are more likely to find conflict and disharmony between family members. This was certainly present in the Tibor case, and may well have been in the Hilda case, Hilda having arrived on the day that the aunt's family moved into a new house, which does seem inopportune. He was very happy at the amazing coincidence of finding a second case on his doorstep where his theory seemed to work. And it did not occur to him that it actually works just as well, and with more sense, if, rather than unplugging a sympathetic relationship, you remove a source of friction.

So far I have touched only on physical phenomena, but it is not just in that area that we see effects following the expectations of their originator, but not persisting in the hands of replicators. This was very evident in the decline of the ESP card based experimental methodology originated by J B Rhine in the 1930s. Rhine discounted the traditional way of studying ESP – by locating a gifted psychic who could give consistent demonstrations of psi cognition – on the grounds that psi-deniers who pride themselves on their intellectual rigour will, on principle, reject all testimony, including that of highly respected scientists, if those luminaries testify to demonstrations of psi by one special subject who, they argue, might well be cheating in some way (and who would in any case soon be dead and his demonstrations dead with him). In that contention Rhine was entirely correct; that is the way of the world, and it will ensure that relatively few people in every generation will be motivated to become immersed in the findings and implications of psychical research. His contention was that the only way to convince such people would be if you could tell them to assemble any group of people: give them a simple test, and you will find that they can demonstrate psi.

Does that sound plausible? Rhine reasoned that for every great mathematician there were people who could add up a column of petty cash, so for every master psychic almost everyone had an iota of psi ability, and, on a statistical basis, it would show up without fail if people were given a sufficient number of simple trials in tests where the right response had a fixed probability. The pack of ESP cards with their five symbols has become iconic, and the testing of single persons or groups of people with targets that are either right or wrong has spread through the world as the procedure identified with parapsychology. To by-pass the impressive effects demonstrated by virtuoso psychics in favour of effects so small that they had to be evaluated by statistics, was probably the most revolutionary idea that anyone has had in the history of psychical research, and, since it took hold on researchers and on the consciousness of the wider world, the virtuoso psychic prepared to demonstrate in controlled experiments has all but ceased to exist. The zeitgeist was, and is, against them, and, in my speculations, the zeitgeist, the prevailing mindset, can have a strong influence over what people can and can't do, and things that happen or don't happen.

Card guessing did produce very positive results in the early years – if eight correct responses out of twenty-five are given when five are expected by chance, and this average is kept up for 100 runs of twenty-five trials, the odds against this being due to chance are very impressive, and the surplus over chance expectation constitutes the evidence that the surplus hits were mediated by psi. At first Rhine, and others following his lead, obtained very good results with this procedure, though, in fact, the best scores were achieved by a handful of named individuals; but, as the years went by, the scores went down. Guessing five symbols was a mind-numbing activity and, after some time (and diminishing returns), various more imaginative methodologies burgeoned, making the trials resemble games, and, with modern technology, hundreds of trials can be laid on rapidly to build up statistical strength. And while statistically significant results continue to pour in, usually relying on large numbers, the actual surplus of hits tends to go down rather than up, and, far from participants improving their receptivity as they get practice, persistence in the same technique tends to bring diminishing returns.

In more recent times we have all been intrigued by the inventiveness of Prof. Daryl Bem, who ran a standard psychology priming experiment backwards, and was rewarded for his creativity by getting the same sort of result as when running it forwards in the usual way (Bem 2011). When a priming experiment is run in the usual way, i.e. with the priming items displayed before the test is run, the experiment makes good sense. People who have been given prior sight of certain words or images will react to them more positively than when shown words or images they have not seen before. Reversing the procedure, they ought not to react to the primed material, because they have not yet been primed – they will get the priming after the test. But his students did what Bem wanted them to do. It was his original idea, and it suggests the possibility of precognition, foresight of the future. Time has passed, and running experiments backwards has been replicated by a considerable number of researchers to a high degree of significance (Bem 2016); it remains to be seen how enduring this procedure will prove to be, and whether the scientific community will ever respond by acknowledging its implications.

When it comes to hostile replicators they can usually be relied on to produce a negative result. An ironical situation arose when noted psi-denier Prof.Richard Wiseman laid on a test for the dog Jaytee, made famous by Dr Rupert Sheldrake as the dog who knew when his owner was coming home (Sheldrake 1999). By the criteria set in Wiseman's scenario the dog failed the test, as trumpeted to the press and lapped up by journalists; but what he didn't notice, and didn't bargain for, was that by the more relevant criteria of the much more extensive series of experiments run by Sheldrake, the dog managed to evade Wiseman's bane and continued to know when his owner was coming home, probably because the co-originator of the test was his owner, who continued to be the key player so far as the dog was concerned (Sheldrake 1999). The press took no interest in that item of corrective news.

So to what extent do people make things happen? It's not a new idea. It has often been remarked that the patients of Jungian analysts dream Jungian dreams, and those of Freud's school produce Freudian ones; in the Maimonides dream laboratory, Montague Ullman's dreamers obliged by dreaming other people's imagery (Ullman 1973), while the followers of Dunne dreamed of future events (Dunne 1927). These things were, of course, within the personal control of people reacting to suggestion, and the idea of making external things happen is a big jump, more readily maintained in the case of experimental work than in spontaneous cases, where we think of things as happening to us rather than of our manipulating things and people and events.

But, we know that psychokinesis is a real effect; if tables can be made to move by PK in séances then, with enough self-belief and determination, originators may also nudge things, in the course of normal life, down a preferred path; and it may take no more effort than that famous butterfly wing-flap. Just a whisper sent from Wratnik's unconscious (but responsive) telepathic circuits to those of Hilda's mother that it would be a nice idea to send Hilda to stay with her aunt, and let Hilda's room to tourists for the summer ... it might be all that was needed to start things moving. And Hilda, willy nilly, and perhaps nilly, went to stay in the country with her young aunt, at a rather stressful time.

But whatever powers might be ascribed to originators I am sure that once the idea has gone off the boil, replicators would not have the same impetus, whether fomenting a poltergeist or inducing a group of people to help sustain a methodology or confirm a theory. As with other creative arts, short of a new angle or some form of personal input, replication does not fire the imagination, and things fade unless they get a fresh coat of paint. It might be a good thing for psychical research if we were to declare robustly that observable paranormal events are not replicable any more than are the individuals who precipitate them.

PUTTING THE HORSE
BEFORE THE CART

~

Telepathy has usually been seen as a faculty manifested by mental mediums (and occasionally by any one of us), and the agent, the presumed source of the telepathic material, is assigned the role of accompanist to the prima donna.

This may be a fair appraisal of the role of a medium who is asked to contact a dead communicator; she, apparently, exercises a radar-like faculty to detect and engage the attention of the designated person. The alternative is that 'the eager dead'[7] may be striving to communicate with the sitter, and profits by finding him or her in the presence of a medium; but, on the living side of the border, all credit must go to the medium for responding. Once contact has been made, the initiative passes to the communicator, but (assuming that the communicator is an entity independent of the medium and the sitter) the communicator's role does not lend itself readily to investigation, the dead being literally beyond our ken.

To study the role of agent we must, therefore, look to the living, and here there are two possibilities. One is to look at the agent in experiments, and the other is to look at the agent in real life situations. So far as experimental work is concerned there are two big problems: one, that there is no way of isolating a telepathic duet from the solo performance of a clairvoyant, because, as has been noted before, clairvoyance cannot be excluded from any experimental procedure involving a target that exists outside the mind of the agent.

---

[7] This nice description of communicators who strive to contact the living was coined by Prof. Archie Roy, one time SPR President.

The other, equally insuperable, is that with trials that rely on statistical assessment, you can never be sure which trial result (i.e. guess) was due to psi and which was due to chance. Even when quality of correspondence in a matching experiment is assessable, the high quality of a response is not a sure guide. If the percipient in an experiment (such as the person attempting to draw an image being viewed by the agent) is later presented with four pictures, one of which was the target, and asked to pick the one that best matches his drawing, he may succeed by choosing, out of four very unpromising possibilities, the one that is the least bad match; contrariwise, he may fail to pick the correct match because, as chance would have it, there happens to be, among the decoy pictures, one that is an equally good match as the true target, and he has chosen that one.

So, to examine the role and contribution of the agent, we do better to look at spontaneous cases, and the ideas proposed here are based on the implications of the rich store of real life telepathic experiences in which telepathy is a much more likely explanation than coincidence, and there is no target that has been exposed outside the mind of the agent. And, while mediums usually report having such experiences, so, occasionally, do members of the public who otherwise have no reason to consider themselves psi-prone. The one-off telepathic experience may take by surprise someone who has hitherto assumed that such things just do not happen; some people to whom this does nevertheless happen allow their minds to be changed, while others tend to bury the memory in the mists of time, and say that nothing funny ever happens to them.

Preliminaries out of the way, I must say that in what follows I have made certain assumptions now to be laid out as axiomatic. The first of these is the familiar one that minds are in an oceanic sort of telepathic linkage, so that in the sub-basement of our unconscious we have a vast amount of material that originated in the minds of others. Further, that our brains block this material from rising into consciousness, shielding us from a state of massive confusion. Above the sub-basement, at a level that might be called the lower ground floor, there is an area in which material immediately relevant to our personal concerns may be elevated into some level of consciousness. The telepath captures this material before it sinks down to the depths.

So the telepath has something akin to sharp hearing. We can all, to some extent, hear our name spoken in the midst of a jumble of background chatter; the telepath has acute psychic hearing. I see this ability as having the same sort of relationship to most people's negligible psychic response as calculating prodigies and pi decimal place memorisers have to people with average arithmetical aptitudes and memories. Conceptually this is fairly simple and, if not totally acceptable as a description of telepathic reception, then it is at least plausible. More complex and fundamentally psi-related issues arise when we turn the spotlight on the initiator at the other end of the interchange, the agent.

In real life it seems clear that it is bad news which gets picked up by telepaths. No one seems to report sudden unexplained feelings of radiant joy and finds later that at that ecstatic moment his twin has just discovered that he has won the national lottery. It is threats of death, accident, pain, anxiety and shock (especially shock) that seem to evoke a telepathic response, whether the response is awareness of a situation, a hallucination, a community of sensation (e.g. inexplicable pain that occurs at the moment that the agent suffers some unexpected trauma), a sense of panic, an urge to take action or just a sinking feeling.

Who is responsible for this linkage of mental states? I would dismiss the idea that the unconscious mind of the ordinary citizen is constantly roving around, telepathically seeking out sad tidings from family and friends. It is far more convincing to assume that the occasional telepath is in a neutral state, and is alerted by the attention-seeking urgency of the personal transmission initiated by the agent. The occasional telepath may see a vision of his dying dog, or may feel as if he is having a heart attack or drowning, or hear a voice summoning her home, or just know that something bad has happened; whatever the nature of the telepathic communication, the telepath is having the contents of his mind modified by signals projected from the mind of the distant agent.

The conveyance of information, sensations or feelings are not the only phenomena involving agents operating remotely. Experiments carried out in France were witnessed by Myers,[8] who wrote an extensive report on what he called hypnosis à distance. The French hypnotists did not hesitate to commandeer their servants to take the role of hypnotic subjects, and, perhaps because of this relationship, the material projected into their minds mostly consisted of orders, which were faithfully obeyed. Were all these servants natural telepaths, as well as being receptive to hypnosis? It seems very unlikely. It looks more as if they were having material forcibly impelled into a level of mind where it was effective to influence behaviour though the hypnotees were not

---

[8]   F W H Myers was one of the SPR founding members and author of the seminal *Human personality and its survival of bodily death*.

aware that the order had been delivered. After several experiences of this sort, the servant might later deduce that the reason she had just performed some pointless action must be because the professor was playing around with hypnosis again. I am not aware that experiments of this sort have been carried out elsewhere, and it is not clear how far the natural subordination of the subject is necessary to secure such ready compliance with telepathic command; but it may well be that telepathy is more closely identifiable with the issue of a command than is generally suspected.

Another activity with links to psi and to hypnosis is distant healing, in which either the patient accepts orders to act on her own physiology or the healer acts directly on the patient's body, this commonly being assumed to be the modus operandi in experiments (usually at close quarters) with animals, insects, plants and micro-organisms. It is not just psi in a general way that is involved in healing, whether hands on or at a distance; it is surely first cousin to the telepathic command reported by Myers. The successful healer is delivering commands to the unconscious mind/autonomic systems of the patients. There is a mechanism that fits all these activities, and that is the psi process generally considered to be in a class well separated from telepathy, and that is psychokinesis – PK.

PK is usually associated with strictly physical effects on objects rather than organisms, and, indeed, some of the best-known early experiments in PK consisted in pushing steel balls around. The term, and the ideas it embodies, actually covers effects on atomic particles to the lifting aloft of tables and other heavy articles. When it comes to modifying the behaviour or bodies of biological entities, the language used is hypnosis, healing and (for the lesser organisms) Dmils (Direct mental interaction with living systems). The word 'mental' does respect the difference between organic and inorganic forms, but it seems to me that in their essentials all these influences are delivered by PK, acting on the brain/mind of the subject, acting on its configurations essentially in the same way as it acted on steel balls to influence the curves they made when they rolled down a slope. The human receiver who perceives and correctly interprets these modifications is a telepath.

The starting point of this talk was a harmless question about the role of the agent in a telepathic episode. The arrival point has been to propose that the agent projects flagged material into a region of the receiver's subconscious from which it can be recovered by a sensitive telepath. This idea may meet with resistance, but at least a consideration of the relationship between agent and telepath must establish that the agent is a main player and key figure. Which was to be demonstrated.

CLAIRVOYANCE AND TELEPATHY

~

The distinction between telepathy (mind to mind transmission/fusion of ideas or sensations) and, on the other hand, clairvoyance (remote perception of things), is a topic I have raised before, and will probably do so again. Clairvoyance and telepathy tend to travel together within the embrace of ESP, but, though both are fairly characterised as extra sensory perception, they are actually not at all alike in how they function.

I used to think that there was only one psychic who, in his time, survived testing to destruction without being destroyed, and that was Stefan Ossowiecki, whose career spanned the end and the beginning of the two European wars. As this Polish clairvoyant is to figure frequently in the following pages it may help to know that his name is pronounced Oss-off-yet-ski. It rolls easily off the tongue once you get used to it. But recently the clairvoyance of a clairvoyant who flourished a century earlier, Alexis Didier, has become more familiar through the works of Prof. Bertrand Méheust (Méheust 2005), and it looks as if Alexis, as he was usually known, stands alongside Ossowiecki as a psychic who demonstrated paranormal cognition repeatedly to all and sundry, including some very critical investigators, and often under well-controlled conditions.[9] Considering aspects of the Alexis reports from the mid-nineteenth century, and those on Ossowiecki from the twentieth-century inter-war years, one can venture to draw some provisional conclusions about the *modus operandi* of the psychic faculty.

---

[9] The next article describes how Didier convinced the famous magician Jean-Eugène Robert-Houdin that his clairvoyance was real.

I have to start with a brief review of the conclusion I arrived at long ago in the case of Ossowiecki's clairvoyance, based on purposefully varied experimental procedures laid on by his researchers. In the interests of distinguishing clairvoyance from telepathy, some of the experiments were deliberately designed to exclude the operation of telepathy. In these tests the experimenter might ask a third party to act as agent by preparing several target papers, writing a few words or making a drawing on each one. The agent then had to put the specimens into identical envelopes, seal them and pass them to the experimenter, who put them into larger and identical outer envelopes, also sealed. The agent was often not acquainted with Ossowiecki, and did not know the purpose of the request. Under those conditions Ossowiecki, when presented with the target envelopes, would be required to reproduce the targets, and would do this with as much accuracy as if he had been making copies after glancing at the targets in the normal way. Now unless one is going to entertain the most convoluted of arguments, it would seem that, in such a case, Ossowiecki could not have been operating by telepathy because, even if holding the envelope put him in rapport with the agent or the experimenter, neither had any way of knowing which of the targets had been selected. So clairvoyance is clearly indicated.

There is more. Dr Gustave Geley, the principal researcher, sometimes acted as agent himself, usually when he wanted to try a new procedure informally. On one occasion the target consisted of two fish scales wrapped in cotton wool and sealed in a box. Ossowiecki gave an accurate description of the hidden articles – they were roundish, flattish, translucent like mica, but he could not say what they were. When, finally, Geley opened the box and showed him the articles he was none the wiser. However, Geley, present and willing the test to succeed, he knew what they were, but Ossowiecki failed to pick the information from Geley's mind.

There are numerous examples of Ossowiecki giving startlingly accurate descriptions of hidden targets while failing to grasp meanings; when Richet wrote the word TOI (French for 'thee') in capital letters, Ossowiecki said correctly that the T had two little downstrokes on the crossbar of the T, but he interpreted what he saw as 'T Zero 1'. Again we can conclude that Ossowiecki failed to grasp the idea behind the three characters, though this would have been in Richet's mind. It is also relevant that the paper on which the fancy T was written was, throughout the experiment, screwed into a ball and held by Richet in his hand, which is a good reason for holding that Ossowiecki did not just send out a sort of extruded X-ray eye to peer though packaging and hands. In fact Ossowiecki's repertoire extended well beyond four walls. He often had to send his clairvoyant eye out on extended voyages, because he would oblige people by locating missing objects, missing people and missing corpses. To assist him in that sort of task, he nearly always wanted to hold an article connected with the person, place or thing (a psychometric object, like a glove or key). Whether these token objects play an objective role in psychometry experiments, or act as a psychological prop, remains an open question – to be solved, one day, if another psychometrist like Ossowiecki can be found.

Putting all the salient facts together I have theorised that Ossowiecki used the target to trace it back in time and so bring himself into contact with the person who created the target, or with the owner of the article, and let it lead him further, as if on a thread, back into that person's past environment, so that he could see the target before it was concealed in an envelope or box. We see both aspects of past-time tracing when he undertook a test with Dr Stephan Chauvet, a physician member of the Institut Métapsychique International (IMI) of Paris, where most of the research with Ossowiecki was carried out. Earlier in the day, Chauvet had asked a patient of his to go into his study and prepare a target, fold the paper, envelope it and seal the envelope, which he intended to put before Ossowiecki that evening at the IMI meeting.

The woman did as asked, but, having dropped hot sealing wax onto the flap of the envelope in two places, she could not find Chauvet's seal, so she hastily used a one-franc coin to seal the wax. Later, the doctor, feeling that this looked rather undignified, dropped more hot wax on the seals and applied his own seal in the form of a Chaldean priest, obliterating the coin images. But when Ossowiecki took the envelope the first thing he talked about was two one-franc pieces, and then he launched into a description of the woman who had created their image, first her appearance, and how he saw her copying a passage from one of Chauvet's books to create the target, but then he went on to her personal history, including her divorce (unusual in the 1920s) and re-marriage. One might say that, having made rapport with the woman, he lifted her life story from her mind by telepathy, but if he could not lift the idea of fish scales from his friend Geley, present and willing, (and while on a fishing expedition) or the idea of Toi from his friend Richet, why should he get reams of biography out of a woman who was not only not present but totally unknown to him?

A notable instance of telepathic failure showed up on that same meeting, when Ossowiecki took a liking to Chauvet and he asked him to provide a personal target. Chauvet, who was in constant pain from an old war wound, went aside and drew a crucifix, and wrote under it 'Ma vie' (My life), meaning it was a life of suffering. The writing was a scrawl, impossible to read (apart from being concealed inside a closed envelope). Ossowiecki drew the crucifix with fair precision, giving it the three-dimensional look that Chauvet had drawn, and he said there was some writing, but he could not read it. And though he knew, presumably from spontaneous telepathic sympathy, that Chauvet had a painful neck wound, he did not, as part of his task, get help from telepathy to explain the meaning of the unreadable writing.

Perhaps the supreme example of Ossowiecki's viewing the past but not engaging with the mind of the target creator is to be found in Geley's invisible ink test. Geley wrote a complex sentence copied from Pasteur, and gave it, in a sealed envelope, to Ossowiecki, who discerned that the target writing was made with invisible ink and doubted that he would be able to 'read' it. But he gave detailed and correct accounts of how Geley created the target, including an interruption by a man with conspicuous moustaches, and said he could watch Geley's pen strokes; from this he gave an account of the sentence structure, and the opening words 'It is not a question of. ...' He finally gave up. But, in spite of seeming to look over Geley's shoulder and watch as he took a book down from his shelf and then copied out the passage, Ossowiecki could not use telepathy to get inside Geley's mind.

If one excludes telepathy on these grounds then what emerges from the totality of Ossowiecki experiments is the concept of retrocognitive clairvoyance, by means of which he used the target as a link object to navigate into the past, and he then gained his information by direct observation. There is another factor that gives this idea support: on taking hold of a target envelope, Ossowiecki's frequent practice was to do as he did with Chauvet's target envelope: that is, he would lead up to his description of the target by talking about the circumstances in which it came into existence, frequently describing not only the agent but also the house, the room, the furnishings, the time of day, other people who were in the room when the target was created, where the agent looked, where they sat, and so on. It is as if he were running a rather blurred videotape back and forth until he could make it freeze or at least hover round the origin of the target.

The retrocognitive element in Ossowiecki's clairvoyance is also strongly indicated when the target had been defaced or destroyed by the time he was asked to reproduce it, so that, in its discernable state, it did not exist in the present. If this is his method of information retrieval when the target has ceased to exist, it seems to me very likely that this is the mode of operation even in cases where the target remains in existence, and even when Ossowiecki's apprehension is very rapid. In some cases the past may be very recent indeed; after all, the past starts the moment the present instant is over. It is all we know. If clairvoyance is essentially a scanning of the past, my further speculation is that telepathic impressions are conveyed in the elusive instant of the present moment, and Ossowiecki certainly did have some flashes of spontaneous telepathic cognition, though they appeared to arrive unsought and were usually peripheral to the experimental task – he might, for example, tell an astonished agent what he had intended to draw before he created the actual target. And that, in brief, is the case for clairvoyance, or retrocognition, or retrocognitive clairvoyance.

The question that arises for consideration now is whether Alexis Didier operated in the same way. He did the same sort of things as Ossowiecki, reading targets, describing people's lives and houses, locating missing people and objects, and going on psychic travels to places he had never visited. But before looking at the clairvoyance/telepathy question, it is important to remember that Alexis operated as a psychic only when he was put into a hypnotic trance, whereas Ossowiecki only had to put himself into a receptive state, not seemingly far removed from his normal state, and, to all appearances, he was not in a state of self-hypnosis, nor did he ever claim to be so. And Alexis lived from his fees as a clairvoyant, while Ossowiecki demonstrated to oblige his friends, who included generals, archbishops and heads of state, and to help people of all walks in life who came to him in distress. Alexis also helped people in need.

Another factor to bear in mind was that Ossowiecki was an engineer and industrialist, and may, therefore, have had a brain that inclined him to visual-spatial imagery rather than to empathy, whereas Alexis, when he was not operating as a psychic, was a part-time actor, and presumably more in rapport with people and their emotions than with things and shapes. If one wants to test the generality of Ossowiecki's *modus operandi* then it is serendipitous that Alexis had such a contrasting personality and lifestyle.

Bertrand Méheust's book on Alexis runs to more than 600 pages, but I am going to draw on a a few samples of material taken from the even longer work by the same author, *Somnambulism and Mediumship* (Méheust 1995). In 1847 the writer Alexandre Dumas wrote two open letters to La Presse, and it is the unusual events described in the second letter that constrained me to compare and contrast Alexis with Ossowiecki. On that occasionAlexis attended Dumas's social gathering without his mesmerist, causing widespread disappointment, the assumption being that without M. Marcillet to put him into a trance state there would be no mesmerism, no somnambulism, and therefore no mediumship. While Alexis and his wife were engaged in relaxed conversation with other guests, a friend of Dumas, one M. Bernard, urged him to mesmerise Alexis himself. Dumas quipped that the only way he could put someone to sleep was by boring him with one of his plays or novels, but Bernard persisted, telling Dumas to forget mesmeric passes and just silently will Alexis to go into trance. So a sceptical Dumas willed it – with the result that Alexis swayed, cried out and collapsed on a sofa with his eyes turned upwards. Dumas, horrified, went over and held his hand, whereupon the entranced Alexis said 'Never do such a thing without warning me; you will kill me.' However, he recovered, and gave demonstrations of mediumship no less sensational than usual.

But, before coming to the clairvoyance, what about the hypnotic induction? Dumas was at pains not to give any outward sign that he was trying to influence Alexis; he had expressed the fear that he would look a fool if he tried and failed, so Bernard told him not to show in any way that he was directing his mind to Alexis. Despite the people involved being in the same room, I doubt very much that sensory clues could have conveyed to Alexis that Dumas was making a preposterous attempt to mesmerise him by remote control and without making any of the usual passes. So this seems to be a case of telepathic hypnosis, and the effect on Alexis, as if he had been struck by a blow, is essentially a case of immediate agent/respondent mind-to-mind telepathy, bearing no resemblance to the solo fishing around and target retrieval activity of retrocognitive clairvoyance. It seems to have been effective on two levels: on one, Alexis knew what had been done to him and by whom, and, on the other, he responded to the order to go into a trance state, responding to telepathic command (as intimated in the previous article).

Alexis's party piece demonstration, guaranteed to strike investigators dumb, was to win card games while blindfold and without turning over his cards, but he became bored with that and passed on to the more human-centred psychometry. Presented now with a ring by a M. Collin, he told the sitter that it had been given to him by a woman aged thirty-five. This sort of thing strongly resembles Ossowiecki's retrocognition with Chauvet. Collin confirmed that this was correct, and asked where the woman was now. Alexis's response was very interesting. He said, "Please try to agree about this with M. Dumas before I can continue. He takes me to America but you want to keep me in Paris".

Dumas explains:

"Around 1844 I had often seen an American lady on Collin's arm. I assumed that the ring came from her. So I pulled Alexis to New York despite efforts by Collin to keep her in Paris".

Dumas then took Collin into another room, where he learned that the lady in question was not the American, but a French woman who lived in Rue St. Apolline in Paris.

Stopping there, it looks as if Alexis was receiving telepathic messages from Dumas and Collin, and was aware of this with startlingly clarity; he was not just confused, he knew exactly what was the source of the confusion. But it is not necessarily so. It seems clear that it was not only rings and gloves and target envelopes that functioned for Alexis as psychometric objects, but people also functioned in this way, just as they did for Ossowiecki, who would astonish strangers by relating their life history. Both of them, but especially Alexis, liked to hold the sitter's hand while doing this, much as they would hold a ring or a pair of gloves. So tracing back in their past experience could lead him to Dumas's observation of the American and Collin's relationship with the French woman. And while retrocognitive backtracking might mean laborious navigation, like moving from link to link on the internet, it might also be very rapid, as in the immediate recall of an event from the distant past. My guess would be that Alexis was time-tracing with Collin and received telepathic interference from Dumas, who, as his mesmerist, would be in a special relationship with him while he remained entranced.

The two men then returned to Alexis, now of one mind, and Alexis said that he found himself in a road bordering the Boulevard, but said he did not know the name of the road. Dumas told him to look at the street sign on the corner of the road, whereupon he said something of considerable interest to our inquiry, which was: "I'd rather read it in your mind".

By whatever means he used, he then named Rue St. Apolline.

Maddeningly, we don't know whether he did in fact read it from their minds; I strongly suspect that if he had been able to do he would have done it without finding himself in a road that he couldn't name; so again

I suspect that he read the street sign. There is support for this from the following incident, which took place after the arrival of another guest. Dumas went downstairs to greet him and bring him to Alexis. Dumas put the guest's hand into that of Alexis and asked Alexis who he was. Alexis said: This is a man of faith; he's really an excellent Christian. - But what is his profession?

'Doctor.' = You're wrong, Alexis.

'Oh, I know what I mean. There are doctors for the body and doctors for the soul. This gentleman is a doctor of souls. He is a priest. ...' [he was, by the way, dressed as a gentleman, not as a priest] Dumas continued: - Now can you tell us where he carries out his duties?

'Oh, that's easy. It's not far away; it's in a huge building, two or three miles from here. Ah, I see some young men in uniform, buttoned from the collar down to the waist. ... The gentleman is almoner at a military academy. ... - Can you say which one?

Certainly. The name of the college is on their buttons. "Read it, Alexis".

'It's Collège St. Cyr.'

There was no talk here about reading minds, and the concept of his place of work in the mind of the priest or of Dumas is not likely to have taken the form of an inscription on the cadets' buttons. So we have what looks very much like an Ossowiecki style exercise in clairvoyance.

If I may interject here, readers unfamiliar with Alexis may think that perhaps he knew M. Collin, his lady friend and the street where she lived, and that he was also previously acquainted with the priest. But you have to multiply this sort of performance by a factor of hundreds or even thousands, and then you probably come to the conclusion that Alexis could not have known salient facts about everyone, and not everyone could have been claiming to meet him for the first time when they already knew him. Some sitters tried to confuse Alexis by thinking or willing him to give the wrong answer to a target problem; but he appeared to ignore the attempted misdirection. In this case Alexis picked up the intruding thought from Dumas, and knew whose thought it was; this is psi of extraordinary accuracy, and suggests the possibility that the rapport between hypnotist and hypnotic subject may be more of a telepathic bond than is commonly supposed.

An Alexis and an Ossowiecki seem to offer themselves for research about once in 100 years. Others may well lurk in the world using their gifts but remaining unknown to research – and in a later article the psychic powers of one Mrs Costello will be displayed. I have an idea that we may have missed such a person not so long ago right in our midst. Prof. Gilbert Murray, the classical scholar, could go into a distant room while his family decided on a target, which they had to speak out loud, however quietly – it might be a title like 'the Merchant of Venice' or an incident, like 'the time we took a picnic at Runnymede' or whatever. Murray was nearly always able to identify the target, homing in on it by stages much like Ossowiecki with a visual target; and, just as Ossowiecki required a written target, or an actual object for his clairvoyance to operate, Murray had to have words spoken (Murray 1916/18). Unfortunately the researchers of the day treated his demonstrations as a game and very readily acceded to the idea that Murray had superauditory powers. But I suspect that supersensory hearing is a legend, that Murray definitely did not childishly sneak back and listen at the keyhole, and that we have here another example of sensory material which, once exteriorised, whether visually or orally, can be accessed by retrocognition, but seldom if ever by telepathy.

So, coming to a brief conclusion: to a large extent the retrocognition demonstrated by Ossowiecki can be seen as also the principal target retrieval process used by Alexis. But in the case of Alexis there are clearer demonstrations of telepathic reception, the most dramatic one being Dumas's induction of a trance state by distant hypnosis. All indications are that experimental tasks were carried out volitionally, even laboriously, by clairvoyance across time, while telepathy operates spontaneously and instantaneously.

DISHONEST DISBELIEF –
A CASE HISTORY

~

lexis Didier, by now a fairly familiar figure, was born in 1826 and died sixty years later in 1886. He flourished mainly in the decade between 1840 and 1850, and the encounter between Alexis, the clairvoyant, and Jean-Eugène Robert-Houdin, the celebrated magician, took place in 1847. But with the dishonest disbeliever, one Michel Seldow, we reach quite recent times. Didier was usually referred to as Alexis, partly because he started practising as a clairvoyant when he was just sixteen-years-old, and partly because his brother Adolphe also practised in the same line, but Alexis was the more gifted. Before saying more, let me mention that all the material related here about Alexis has been gleaned from *Un Voyant Prodigieux* by Bertrand Meheust, and his *Somnambulism et Médiumnité*; neither, sadly, is published in English (Méheust 2005, 1995).

To call Alexis gifted would be an understatement, and prodigious is not an overstatement, because if psychics were given artistic ratings in the same way as other creative artists, then, as the feats performed chez Alexandre Dumas indicated, Alexis would be one of the few in the genius class. At that gathering he talked informally with people met on a social occasion, but at other times he was tested under more formal conditions and by experienced researchers, and the extraordinary quality of his clairvoyance under test needs to be appreciated to make it worth exploring the lengths to which psi-deniers will go to discredit genuine demonstrations of paranormal cognition.

If Alexis had practised fifty years later then we should expect to have reports from members of the SPR whose names are familiar to us, because he gave sessions in England as well as in France. But creditworthy investigators existed before 1882, when the SPR was founded, and there were publications that dealt with the less frequented corners of inquiry about the nature of reality. One of these was *The Zoist*, the editor of which was Dr. John Elliotson, a professor of medicine at University College. Elliotson was a man of great integrity, who actually ruined his career by persistently supporting the claims made for mesmerism. It was very appropriate that *The Zoist* should have published a report about Alexis, because Alexis's mediumship manifested solely when he was put into a mesmeric trance – magnetised, to use the contemporary description.

Today a hypnotic state is usually evidenced by sticking needles into the entranced person, or telling him he can't raise or lower his hand, or making him dance with a broomstick or forget the number seven, in other words by exhibiting the hypnotist's power over him; but, strange as it now seems, in the early nineteenth century mesmeric trance was more likely to be proved by the subject giving demonstrations of clairvoyance. That clairvoyance, a disputed psi faculty, should be taken to prove the existence of what we should call hypnotic trance state – one generally accepted as real – is a historical anomaly that arose because the early 'magnetisers' were interested in healing patients rather than exercising power over them, and they noticed that when deeply magnetised, the patients became clairvoyant, starting to talk about things that were happening in other places. Alexis, who always needed to be mesmerised to become clairvoyant, was in fact called a 'somnambule,' a somnambulist, rather than a clairvoyant, the psychic gift being so identified with the mesmerised state.

The report from which I am going to quote to show what Alexis could do for an experienced investigator was sent in to *The Zoist* by a friend of Elliotson, the Rev. Chauncey Hare Townsend, who had a session with Alexis in 1851 while Townsend was visiting Paris. Usually Alexis was mesmerised by Jean-Bon Marcillet, his mentor and business partner in the clairvoyant enterprise, but, as Townsend was himself a mesmerist, Marcillet on this occasion let Townsend take over, and left him alone with Alexis as soon as he was satisfied that Townsend had succeeded in putting Alexis into a mesmeric trance. This, at a stroke, eliminates the inevitable mutterings that Marcillet, who had, in any case, met Townsend for the first time an hour or two earlier in the evening, was prompting Alexis.

Another factor that can be eliminated is that Alexis spent the previous night researching the life of Townsend, because the session took place within a few hours of this meeting, and with no interval between the two events. Marcillet caught Alexis on his way home from the theatre, and secured his agreement to an immediate session, as Townsend was leaving Paris the next day. Townsend had a cautious attitude to Marcillet and Alexis, which was fully justified, bearing in mind that they both made a comfortable living from Alexis's demonstrations, and before his own encounter Townsend was more than half inclined to assume that Alexis was a trickster – but not afterwards.

Townsend's report on this encounter runs to eight pages, out of which I shall pick some highlights to give the flavour of a session with Alexis. He started by asking Alexis to use his distant viewing faculty to visit Townsend's house. 'Which one?' Alexis asked. 'You have two, one in London and another in the country.' Townsend specified the country house. Alexis gave a very good description of the exterior of the house and the garden, which were not a typical English country house and garden, because they were in Italy; but it is not until we get to the interior that things become precise beyond any possibility of cold-reading guesswork.

Alexis said he saw a lot of pictures on the walls of the living room, all modern except two; of those two he said that one was a seascape and the other had a religious theme. At this point Townsend says that he felt a frisson, because Alexis's description was absolutely right; that was enough for a frisson, but then Alexis continued. 'There are three figures in this painting, an old man, a woman and a child. Is it the Virgin Mary? No, she is too old. The woman has a book on her knees, and the child is pointing to something in the book. And there is a distaff in the corner.' Townsend confirmed that the painting represented St. Anne teaching the Virgin Mary to read, and there was a distaff (a yarn-winder) in the corner.

Townsend then asked what the picture was painted on. After some thought Alexis said it was on stone; he said he would examine the back, and then said that it was grey or nearly black. Townsend says that the picture was in fact painted on black marble. But Alexis was not finished. 'Hello,' he said 'It's concave.' If Townsend had felt a shiver before, it was this detail that must have had him weak at the knees, because the black marble was indeed concave, and had presented a big problem for the framer.

Visiting the town house Alexis gave a very full description of a Grinling Gibbons mirror in the drawing room above the mantelpiece. 'The mirror' he said 'is small in comparison with the frame. The frame has flowers, fruits, and other sculptured features.' Then suddenly he said 'I can see a portrait reflected in the mirror ... the woman has a red flower on her dress; she is wearing black or rather dark brown. There are two children. It's another religious subject, a holy family.' He then correctly identified the painting as a Raphael, and Townsend confirmed that the name of Raphael appeared on the painting. Alexis went on to give a full description of the paintings on each side of the Raphael, one of a storm at sea and the other a painting by Morland, the interior of a stable, showing a man with a wheelbarrow and a grey horse lying down. All correct in every detail, including the remark that the poor horse has a sore on his back. And on it goes. This is a sample of a sample, and it is by no means the most sensational of reports about Alexis.[10] Faced with demonstrations of this sort the introduction of a skilled magician seems fairly otiose, for what sort of conjuring could enable Alexis to describe an ornate mirror in Townsend's house and the portrait reflected in it, and the pictures on each side of the portrait. The only plausible theory would be that far from putting Alexis into a hypnotic trance, Marcillet would put all sitters into that state and make them imagine the whole sitting. But I must be careful: words uttered in jest may turn up as a fully-fledged denialist theory one day. It has happened. Nevertheless, people have always held the opinion of magicians in high regard, and, in 1847, some four years before the encounter with Townsend a very wealthy and eccentric demonologist, the Marquis de Mirville, commissioned the sceptical Robert-Houdin to attend a sitting with Alexis as an expert and give him a written report and opinion.

De Mirville does not mention the offer of a fee, but there may have been an understanding between them on this point. De Mirville stated only that Houdin was delighted to accept the invitation, asking if he could bring his wife with him. Houdin had been responsible for unmasking a somnambulist called Prudence, and he had declared that all somnambulists (meaning mesmerised clairvoyants) were frauds. He was not expecting to change his mind.

And so to de Mirville's account of the sitting attended at his request by Houdin. Sittings with Alexis often started with his being blindfolded and performing various feats such as playing a game of cards, which he always won. On this occasion Houdin arranged the blindfold himself

---

[10] Townsend's report and other material relating to Alexis is available through the SPR online library.

and then, using his own pack, laid out ten cards on the table, face down, which, to his great surprise, Alexis named correctly. Houdin checked the blindfold and the test was repeated, three times, with the same result, causing Houdin to turn pale and utter bewildered exclamations. Houdin then removed the blindfold, which didn't seem to be doing anything useful, and took a book from his pocket, asking Alexis to cite some words from two-thirds the way down page eight. Alexis quoted the words 'after this sad ceremony.' At this point there was a notable 'failure' of mediumship – because those words in that sequence were actually written two-thirds the way down the adjoining page nine.

I shall not give every detail of this sitting, but it can be said that Alexis succeeded in every other test given to him, including some more interesting items than simple down-through clairvoyance. He identified a hair as belonging to Houdin's son, and gave some assurances about the boy's state of health. He identified the writer of a letter handed to him by Houdin, and told him, to Houdin's immediate annoyance, that the friend who had written the letter was engaged in an act of treachery against him. We shall hear the outcome of that later. When the sitting was over, Houdin said to de Mirville that if he knew a trickster who could perform marvels such as those of Alexis he would admire him even more as a trickster than as an agent of the unknown.

Houdin kept his word to the Marquis: He subscribed to de Mirville's report the following attestation: ' ... I am bound to state that the facts reported above are absolutely correct and that, the more I think about it, the more impossible is it for me to class them among the activities that comprise my art and works.'

De Mirville continued to relate that two weeks after that memorable sitting he received a letter from Houdin dated sixteenth of May 1847, in which Houdin described how he had attended a further sitting with Alexis, this time bringing with him a friend of 'calm judgment.'

Houdin says that on this occasion he took even more stringent precautions, and the results were more miraculous than at the first sitting. To quote: '... And it leaves me in no doubt as to the clairvoyance of Alexis.'

He went on to describe a bizarre game of cards in which Alexis made it clear that he knew the identity of the cards that would turn up for his own hand, and he also knew the cards held by Houdin and clutched in his hand under the table. Houdin doesn't say who won, but as Alexis advised him about which cards he should play it doesn't make much difference. In capital letters Houdin wrote: 'I came away from that sitting as amazed as it is possible to be, and convinced that it is absolutely impossible that either chance or sleight of hand could ever produce such wonderful effects.' It does sound, doesn't it, like a ringing endorsement, one that would be impossible to turn round and represent as a dismissive put-down – but the devices of the psi-denier are boundless, as we shall see.

Houdin himself left the psi-denier a window of opportunity, because, though he published various works after those two encounters, he refrained from making any reference to Alexis, and that window was opened wide by Michel Seldow in a book published in 1971 entitled *Vie et secrets de Robert-Houdin*. The meeting with Alexis and subsequent reports are dealt with in a section curiously and inaccurately entitled 'Robert-Houdin and the phantoms. The author finds himself painfully poised on Morton's fork, because, while he would not attribute any discreditable agenda to his hero, Houdin, he apparently could not live with the idea that Houdin had truly endorsed the clairvoyance of Alexis. So how did Michel Seldow propose to airbrush Houdin's words of support out of history? By a number of inconsistent theories.

One was that any correct statements made by Alexis were due to chance; another was that any tests successfully met were the fruits of chicanerie; yet another that there was such a high degree of inaccuracy in the results that there was really nothing to explain. Seldow would be demeaning Houdin if he were to suggest that he had been taken in by Alexis, so, while assuming that Marcillet was obviously assisting Alexis in fraud, he does not propose any methodology. He would have had quite a problem in succeeding where Houdin himself had failed. And was the master magician incapable of fitting an effective blindfold? Or placing cards face down? Or holding the cards under the table?

And what about the book-reading, the book being held closed by Houdin throughout. Ah – well, Alexis did have to touch the book, and rub his hand over it. Doesn't that show that citing a phrase to be found on page eight was a trick? But the rather inconsistent clinching stroke from Seldow is that the phrase that should have been on page eight was actually on page nine, showing that, regardless of the trick involved in touching the book, the test was a total failure. The words 'after this sad ceremony' that were found two-thirds the way down page nine might, he asserts, be on any page in any book that you happened to pick up at random. Either way, there was no clairvoyance, and when de Mirville talks about the look of stupefaction on Houdin's face this was, in fact, the look of a man who was with difficulty restraining himself from breaking out into laughter. (I'm not making this up).

The crucial problem for Seldow was, of course, how to get round those clear statements of support. His solution was, one has to concede, imaginative. He declares that Houdin did not mean what he had said. Now why would that be? Seldow's answer is that he was telling De Mirville a fairy tale to make him happy, poor mad Marquis, and Houdin was in too much awe of the aristocracy to issue a denial when De Mirville published his endorsement of Alexis for all to see. But Houdin is credited with other kindly motives. He was sorry for the two pathetic mountebanks, Alexis and Marcillet, and would not want to deprive two struggling colleagues of their livelihood. The allegedly struggling Alexis was, at the time, a clairvoyant of international renown, and he was making a very good living from his gift, as Houdin well knew. It is indeed fanciful to imagine that the unmasker of the unfortunate Prudence would have been so indulgent to the prosperous duo of Marcillet and Alexis.

So how deferential was Houdin to de Mirville? Sorry for him enough to commit himself to public ridicule if he vouched for clairvoyance that he knew to be fraudulent, and which might be exposed as such at any time? Did he imagine that his expert opinion would remain confidential? That is not how it reads. It is clear that de Mirville wrote a report not for himself but addressed to the world at large, and Houdin's endorsement is not addressed to De Mirville as a private communication but as a confirmation of De Mirville's announcement. And, the sixty-four-thousand dollar question; what about Houdin's letter reporting on his second sitting?

If you can imagine for a moment that after the first sitting, when he had been commissioned to report to De Mirville, Houdin felt obliged to tell the Marquis what he wanted to hear, is it conceivable that having once committed himself to a false position he would seek out a second sitting, and write to De Mirville confirming his first opinion in even stronger terms? For while his first endorsement said in effect that what Alexis did was not conjuring, the second said that Houdin was convinced that Alexis had demonstrated true clairvoyance. Could any reasonable person believe that the second sitting and Houdin's positive verdict on it was written to please de Mirville.

And, of course, de Mirville's report was very rapidly communicated to the world. Within six months the entire text of his account of the sitting and the two statements by Houdin were published, first in the *Revue d'anthropologie catholique*, and then in *la Gazette de France*, where it appeared headlined on the front page. Following this publicity the expert opinion of Houdin was widely cited in publications by mesmerists, doctors and also by psychical researchers in France and in England. In 1854 there it was all again in de Mirville's book *Spirits and their Fluid Manifestation*. Never was there the slightest cautionary hint from Houdin that his statements should not be taken at face value.

But we don't have to rely entirely on publications by de Mirville and the supposed immunity of the aristocrat from contradiction. In 1860, well within Houdin's lifetime, André-Saturnin Morin, a lawyer, politician and writer published a work entitled *Du magnetisme et des sciences occultes* – Mesmerism and the occult sciences – in which he records a personal meeting with Houdin who not only confirmed his earlier statements but added a lot of detail about the sittings he attended. He told Morin about how he had made an amusing hobby out of watching charlatans claiming paranormal powers and then performing the same tricks, but doing them more skilfully; but when de Mirville introduced him to Alexis he was confounded.

Morin relates, in quotation marks, Houdin's account of the blindfolding followed by the card games. He said that what Alexis said to Houdin's wife about the loss of their child was perfectly correct, and that they were stupefied. The most interesting new information to emerge was that there was another person present, a sceptically inclined Dr. Chomel (identified by Bertrand Méheust as probably a prominent member of the Academy of Medicine), who presented a small box to Alexis for psychometry. After feeling it, Alexis said that it contained a medal; 'It was given to you in strange circumstances. You were a poor student, living in a garret in Lyon. A workman you had helped found this medal in the rubbish, thought that you might like it and climbed your six staircases to offer it to you.' All that, said Houdin, was true – hardly details arising by chance or guesswork.

As the presence of Chomel was not mentioned by de Mirville it looks as if either Houdin or Morin conflated the first and second sittings, because Chomel could well fit the description of the friend with sound judgment who Houdin asked to be allowed to bring with him to the second sitting.

The other item of considerable interest is Houdin's statement to Morin about Alexis's warning not to trust the writer of the letter Houdin had given Alexis. Houdin said that he had reacted angrily, but Alexis had persisted. Three months later, Houdin told Morin, the good friend turned out to be treacherous, and he had been trying to get Houdin's assistants to betray his secrets. So Alexis had been right when insisting, against Houdin's protests, that the writer of the letter presented to him was a false friend.

There we have confirmation that de Mirville's narratives were genuine, that Houdin was convinced by Alexis's clairvoyance, and we learn that there was a sterling witness present who also received convincing proofs. So Houdin was not humouring de Mirville; and, far from wanting to burst out laughing, Houdin was duly dumfounded by the clairvoyance of Alexis.

There is one more independent reference to Houdin and his encounter with Alexis. This comes in a book by Maute de Fleurville published in 1873, *Etudes sur le magnetisme* – Studies in Mesmerism. He says that he once heard Houdin say: 'I could teach Alexis my skills, my tricks, and he would learn to perform them as I do ... but never, never could I perform what he does; that is beyond imagination.'

Now all this would presumably be well known to Michel Seldow, and, armed with this knowledge, no reasonable person could postulate that Houdin's testimonials were feigned; but once you are committed to a fundamentalist faith then reason melts away. And no faith seems to unseat reason more thoroughly than the wilder shores of psi-denial. We must not be too polite to denounce this sort of absurdity in the roundest terms. And the roundest term for this sort of argument is not scepticism, with or without a k, but dishonest rubbish.

As to current psi-deniers, especially those who have the ear of the media when purporting to debunk reports of well witnessed phenomena or successful experiments, all one can say is 'Plus ça change, plus c'est la même chose.' They were at it 150 years ago, and they are still at it.

PART THREE:

OPPOSITE ENDS OF A SPECTRUM

INTRODUCTION

~

The contrast between the early British/American approach (head in the clouds) and the French (feet on the ground) has been noted in the introduction. The founders of the SPR in 1882 had the stated aim of investigating the claims of spiritualism, and the energy of the early researchers went into massive efforts to establish the true identity of personages apparently communicating very convincingly through selected mediums. Many of these communications are particularly impressive in seeming to come from dead colleagues who had survived complete with memories, personalities and specialist knowledge intact.

This concentration on survival research remained the dominant aim for about forty years, after which a rather depressing feeling began to take hold that the certainty enjoyed by committed Spiritualists would always elude the critical inquirer. Hope does, of course, spring eternal, and the search for strong evidence continues, while no longer dominating the field. Though the difficulties of eliminating alternative explanations seem to be insuperable, survival or extinguishment is for many people (and perhaps for most who are prepared to think about it) rather literally the matter-of-life-and-death question.

Though a secular country, France is also grounded in Catholicism, which forbids attempts to contact the dead, and this may have had some influence in determining the course of French research. But there was, in fact, a very active Spiritist movement in France, and the aversion of researchers to engaging with them is more likely to have been because the founding of the IMI was post-the 1914 war, so well into the age of science supreme, and very well after the shock felt by Victorians at losing the certainties of religion, including, of course, the resurrection of the dead.

The scientists comprising the IMI wanted to draw the sharpest line between their scientific investigations and what they saw as the childish nonsense of spiritists. Whereas Catholicism frowned on spiritism, English law took a draconian view of claims to foretell the future, judges having proclaimed that as this was impossible any claim to do so for payment would be obtaining money by false pretences, and likely to incur a prison sentence. The French do not seem to have been affected by a similar ruling, and researchers were able to monitor the results of predictions made to sitters inquiring their about business ventures and other worldly matters.

But first we look at some of the more recent inquirers into the other world, or recipients of phenomena they see as revelationary.

THE STRONGEST LINK

~

I had to give this paper a title that would fit on one line, hence the rather enigmatic strongest link. A more ample title would be Three cases quite difficult to explain without postulating an intervention from someone no longer living who forms an essential link in a chain of information sharing. I don't know how much more explanatory that is than the short title, but all will be revealed quite soon.

Though three cases have been selected, the first one will not take long to relate; the second will take more time, and be subjected to a lot of comment, but it is the third one that will take the lion's share and illustrate most strongly the difficulty one would have in proposing an explanation for it entirely in terms of living people, by which I mean people living at the time of the event.

The back-up evidence for my first case is, looked at objectively, quite flimsy; however, I don't look at it objectively, because it was told to me by an SPR member whose word I accept absolutely. Even if you allow for inaccuracies to creep into the telling, I am confident that the core of the story is reliable. It took place in the early 1970s, at a series of sittings with Leslie Flint, which I attended most weeks for nearly a year. He did not do a lot so far as I was concerned personally, but, for mediumship to burgeon, it probably takes two to tango, and I may not figure as a good dance partner.

I have absolutely no memory of hearing the communication in question here, but week after week communicators came through, some who sounded fairly convincing, others who seemed to natter on about nothing of interest. I think I might have written off the communicator in this case as one of the inconsequential natterers, and wiped it from my memory. So my informant, Nigel Buckmaster, may be telling me about something that happened at a sitting I did not attend, or he may be reminding me about something that made no impression at the time.

The sitter who received the communication was his wife, Doreen. Leslie announced that Mildred wanted to speak to Doreen, who responded by saying that she had never known anyone called Mildred. Leslie persisted, and finally said that it was Milly – a name Doreen immediately accepted, and a female sort of voice addressed her (usually the voice that came through this medium purported to be the voice of the deceased communicator). Doreen was in a mood to tease, and she told Milly that when she was alive she would not have approved of communication from beyond – Milly being a fairly convinced Catholic who considered dabbling with spirits to be decidedly sinful.

But Milly had no time for this sort of banter. She told Doreen that she had something important to impart: her younger sister May (Milly's surviving younger sister) was, she said, planning to do something very foolish with her house, and Doreen must stop her. Doreen protested that May lived in Edinburgh while Doreen, who had also been brought up there, had lived in London for the last thirty years, and they were not in touch at all. But Milly had said her piece and was gone.

The background to this was that during Doreen's childhood in Edinburgh, Milly had been old enough to act in a quasi-motherly or auntish role to Doreen, and they had been quite close in that relationship; but Milly's sister, May, was too young to be an aunt but too old to be a friend, and so Doreen had never been close to May, and they had totally lost touch. Doreen had no intention of travelling to Edinburgh to tell May that the deceased Milly had said not to do what she was planning to do with her house – and who can blame her. It was soon water under the bridge.

But ... about a year later a friend from Edinburgh visited Doreen and by way of gossip asked if she had heard about the awful fate that had befallen May. The story was that May had given her house to her nephew, on the understanding that he and his family would move in and look after her for the rest of her days. They started by commandeering her room for themselves and putting her in a less favoured room. Then they decided that looking after her was too much of a chore, and decanted her into a rather nasty local authority home for the aged and indigent – and there she was. Doreen, feeling now that she had neglected a duty cast on her by Milly went up to Edinburgh and, being a forceful woman, moved and shook generally until she got May into quite a nice residential home. There the story ends. You may (if you are desperate to dismiss mediumship) write off the communication from Milly as a lucky hit by the medium, a simple coincidence. But that is not my idea of a sensible response, so I pass on to other questions.

The crucial question I ask myself is how this information about May and her house got to Doreen without some help from Milly. You might – and probably will – speculate that Doreen had heard rumours of May's plans from someone who was acquainted with both of them, such as the one who told Doreen about it after the event. It certainly wasn't from that person, because there was no prior conversation about 'Do you remember I told you what she was planning.' I also think we can forget about the possibility that Doreen could have given the information to Leslie in the course of informal conversation, and it seems evident that Doreen herself had never heard about it before the sitting.

I might add that if Doreen had been told any such rumour, she would certainly have remembered it, because she was a very sharp-witted woman, interested in people, a writer who took note of things said and done, and certainly she would have remembered being told about something of that sort. I am also sure that her husband would have known about it, because they were very much a united team, and when Leslie's communicator talked about May doing something foolish with her house they would surely have remembered that this was not the first time the subject had been mentioned. After the sitting, though she had not intended to take any action, she would have briefed her husband about Milly and May, because they always discussed the sittings, and this communication was very personal to her.

So, assuming there was no normal leakage of information, what about paranormal leakage? Could May, when planning her rash move, have been troubled in her more perceptive subconscious mind and sent out distress signals to be picked up by anyone sensitive to her telepathic cries for wise counsel? Perhaps she had a subconscious precognition of what was going to happen to her, because subdivisions of the mind seem to have lives of their own. But why should Leslie Flint pick up those signals? Could Doreen have acted as a sort of psychometric object, a conduit to significant people and events in her life experience in the same way that personal articles may act on sensitives who touch them? That is a possibility worth some consideration. But then why should Doreen, never close to May and almost a stranger by now, as well as 400 miles away from practical assistance, lead Flint straight to May, who could hardly have been more marginal?

None of these ideas is so grotesque as to be outside the boundaries of paranormal cognition, but I do say that Milly is the one person who binds May and Doreen together, Doreen having been bound to Milly and Milly having been bound to her sister May. So, though survival is always the least economical explanation, a message from Milly to Doreen about May seems, on the face of it, a more plausible explanation than a complex mixture of premonitory telepathy, with psychometry and role creation thrown in. But we know that the face of things can be deceptive, so let's look further.

The next case is one that members may have read about in the SPR Journal correspondence columns, the first hand account being found in a letter from Denise Iredell correcting and amplifying an earlier very brief allusion to her experience by Manfred Cassirer – a rather inadequate forum for what I regard as a very important case, too important on every front to be indexed only under letters to the editor (Iredell 1986). The medium in question is the controversial – in other words much reviled – Helen Duncan, and the SPR member who had the seminal experience was, like the informants in the previous case, someone who could be relied on absolutely to tell the truth as she believed it to be. Of course, people of integrity can be mistaken about what they see or hear, or remember, but, in this case, I don't see much space for mistakes so fundamental as to undermine the case.

Denise Iredell's story dates from 1949, and we are back in Edinburgh, at a time when her mother, Muriel Hankey, was the principal of Edinburgh Psychic College, a Spiritualist organisation. (Later in life Mrs Hankey became an SPR council member for a few years, so she had at least a rather tentative toe in the more sceptical camp). Denise, who was twenty at the time, decided rather suddenly that she would visit her mother before going abroad, so she took a flight to Edinburgh and arrived unannounced. She was met by someone in an official position, and, when he realised that she was Mrs. Hankey's daughter, he told her that there was to be a séance with Helen Duncan that evening and, as there had been a last minute cancellation by a sitter, Denise could, if she liked, attend the séance. She had never attended a Duncan sitting before, and of course she accepted the offer. I mention these details to make it clear that there was little, if any, time in which to research Denise's life between her arrival and the sitting that evening, supposing that anyone was minded to do so.

Denise's description of the sitting is well beyond the boggle threshold of most people, but she was one of the most sensible and level-headed people I have ever met, and I see no rational grounds for not believing that this is what she – and her mother – saw. About twelve to fourteen people sat in a horseshoe circle, and at the open end of the horseshoe was the cabinet (a large sort of wooden sentry box enclosed by a pair of black curtains hanging in front and having an armchair inside for the entranced medium). Denise said that through the crack in the curtains she could see Helen Duncan sitting in the cabinet. After a short time, a tall phantom figure, not at all like Helen Duncan (who was, to speak plainly, short and fat) emerged from the cabinet and stood in front of it to one side. This figure would be recognised by some of the sitters in the circle as 'Albert,' the materialised 'control' personage, who would speak on behalf of the entranced medium and act as master of ceremonies.

Albert, who spoke rather effete English, unlike Mrs. Duncan's almost incomprehensible Scots, would from time to time call out the name of the sitter for whom a communicator was said to be waiting, or describe the communicator in detail, so that some sitter claimed acquaintance; then that person came and stood in the middle of the horseshoe, facing the cabinet. In front of where that person stood there was a red light at high level throwing down a beam of illumination. Denise watched while most of the sitters, one or two at a time, stood in the circle, and, on each occasion, she saw a white substance – so-called ectoplasm – come out of the cabinet, wriggle over the floor to the lit up area in front of the the sitter, rear up into a vertical structure underneath the red light and form itself into the shape of a recognisable human being, swathed in some sort of clothing.

The figure might be a man, or a woman, young or old, and in each case it was greeted by the sitter and they would talk to one another. Denise was a polite girl rather than a researcher, and made a point of not listening to their private conversation – she thought it would be 'intrusive.' Then it was her turn: Mrs Hankey and her daughter were called together, and both stood in the circle – so, I must point out again, in passing, that if one of them had a hallucination, the other had one apparently identical, or similar enough for them to assume that they had seen the same things.

What Denise said she saw was that the column of white stuff was turning into a man, and, as his features formed, she recognised him as a friend of her mother's, who had been a sort of uncle figure to her, though not particularly close. She was struck by his blue eyes, blue in spite of the red light. As she watched he developed a full moustache, and, as she had remembered him with a neat sort of pencil of hair on the upper lip, this surprised her to the point that she exclaimed 'a moustache!' whereupon – and in the midst of this miracle of life apparently triumphing over death we have a heavy touch of farce – he turned to her and said, in his characteristically clipped voice 'Is that all you've got to say?' Abashed, Denise said no more.

I'm afraid that there is no record of the subsequent dialogue between him and Mrs Hankey, so I don't know if it moved to higher planes, but Denise and her mother discussed the materialised figure later, and Muriel showed Denise a photograph of her friend when he was younger than when Denise had known him, and she then saw that he had a full moustache. Now, I must tell you that this is all preliminary, and I cite it for completeness and because I want to show that Denise and her mother agreed about what they had seen, eliminating, in my view, the idea that people at these sittings just gave free rein to their imaginations.

I do not discount the possibility of shared hallucinations, but I should expect that they would have to be precipitated by something more akin to hypnosis, which does not seem to have been present here. As for self-hypnosis, though the materialised visitor was very welcome, neither mother nor daughter had a crying need to renew acquaintance with the family friend.

It is the second materialised phantom that I want to talk about now, because, when the family friend departed, the ectoplasm collapsed into a whitish pool on the floor; but, instead of retreating back into the cabinet as it had done on previous occasions, it stayed on the floor, pulsating, while Albert announced that now there was a visitor for Mrs. Hankey's daughter alone. So Muriel went and sat down, wondering who, if anyone, had died who was known to Denise but not to her. Denise was wondering the same thing, and thought Albert must have made a mistake.

Albert, or anyway the voice, then described the death of what he called 'a young girl' by cancer, and Denise still did not accept that she knew any young girl who had died in this way. She thought about a girl who had died at the age of eight when Denise was around that age herself, but she did not die of cancer. While she was thinking about a child rather than a young woman, the ectoplasm picked itself up and formed itself into a female figure of a young adult, then clarified the features, and then she recognised her as a girl from her own school, but who was somewhat older, and had left the school before Denise went there. This girl, known to us as J., had died the year before in her late twenties, and she had indeed died of cancer.

There was a connection between them: the dead girl had edited the school *alumnae* magazine, and when she died, Denise, who had met her perhaps a dozen times, had taken over over that job. So J. had been an acquaintance rather than a friend, and Denise was not emotionally over-excited to see her visitor. The wonder of it was not so overwhelming to her as it would be to most of us, because she had been brought up to understand that communications from the other side and the occasional materialisation of spirit forms were the sort of thing you expected to happen at sittings, and this reunion did not mean much to her on a personal level. But there the phantom form unmistakeably was, and Denise apologised for not having recognised her at first. J politely said that that was quite all right. There was a little more small talk, the details of which Denise does not remember, except that, crucially, Denise mentioned the nickname of one of the joint headmistresses at their school.

J's reply might have been designed to confirm her identity and show that she had an item of knowledge shared with Denise but not likely to be known by anyone who had not made extensive inquiries into their lives. She said, 'Please give them both my love.' The significance of this response is considerable. Their school was run by joint principals, and, in giving this reply, she showed that she recognised the nickname of one and also knew that she was one of two people in a dual role. However, the point I want to make here is that it was not a message that Denise wanted to hear. Though the headmistresses were fairly open-minded about Spiritualism, Denise was not at all happy about feeling obliged to give them this message from the deceased J. But, being a conscientious person, she duly conveyed the greeting, which was received sympathetically.

Now I regard this whole narrative as evidentially outstanding. The preliminary episode with the family friend establishes for me, and in my view for any open-minded person, that the materialisations were not private delusions. I have also checked with Denise that she discussed the schoolgirl phantom with her mother, who had no inhibitions about taking a good look at Denise's visitor.

It is the appearance of the materialised school friend that discredits all those apparently plausible ideas about how people, fortified with hope and expectation, comfort themselves by creating illusions about life after death and reunion with people they loved and want to see again. Denise was not looking desperately for proof of survival; she had been brought up with that assumption. Nor did she need to convince herself that phantom forms can manifest and talk to people. And as for the girl who materialised, Denise certainly did not seek an encounter with her, and still less did she want to be lumbered with her message. As I see it, this puts paid to the idea that séance room materialisations and communications can be entirely written off as nothing but self-deception induced by wish-dreams and expectant longing.

So, if the episode was not born of wish fulfilment, how might the encounter be explained without some input from the dead girl? She comes over as the initiator, the one who forced her agenda on the sitter. But there are things we must bear in mind before concluding that J's mind was the directing force behind the phantom figure. Because a phantom that walks and talks, looks and sounds like a known person might still be a construct of living minds. How much could the medium have known about J if hers was the mind in question? Mediums often pick up and retain in their memory desultory scraps of information and put them together more coherently than most of us could manage to do by conscious effort. They can get to know a lot about people without even trying, and it may be that medium and sitters act jointly, their unconscious minds combining knowledge with psychic power, and producing a materialisation that pools their inputs.

Muriel Hankey was a Spiritualist mixing freely with others, and, in the course of social conversation, mediums and their friends would get to know a lot about her and her family and her friends. They might, for example, have heard about the family friend, even met him. But would they have known that many years earlier he had worn a full moustache? And would the medium have been able to role-play him, and his voice, so efficiently as to give his sort of response to Denise's exclamation, rather than a more stereotyped response like 'Yes, my child, spirits can change their forms.'

One can apply similar principles to the J episode. This is at one remove, because she was not a friend of Muriel Hankey herself. But mothers often talk about their children, and I should not rule out the possibility that Muriel could have talked about how her daughter had taken over the editorship of the school *alumnae* magazine from an older girl who had died of cancer. But would this sort of social chat have extended to the school's being run by joint principals? And how likely is it that Muriel would have referred to one of the headmistresses by her nickname? Not very, as I see it, and it is J's response to that name that is the telling point.

Assuming that materialisations require some contribution from sitters, Denise had the required information. But, consciously at least, she did not know who was going to materialise until she was recognisable. Once J was identified, Denise could have contributed the detail needed to pursue the conversation leading to the message. It may seem like straining at the gnat to to agonise about living-mind explanations for the mental aspects of the phenomena when you are swallowing the camel of materialisation. But that gnat is a person who has survived death to put in a surprise appearance at a sitting. But perhaps J was as much surprised as Denise, if she was the object of motivation rather than the motivator. Did Denise, through the machinations of her subconscious mind, project the image and personality of the dead girl into the subconscious of the medium, who gave it back in the form of a materialisation? Is that to be preferred to the idea that J was attracted to Denise because of the continuing connection with their school, and hence the school-orientated conversation and message?

School was indeed the nexus, but it is nevertheless curious, to say the least, that J sent her love to her headmistresses but makes no mention of her parents. Is that enough to throw doubt on the true identity of J? We do not know enough about J to warrant a firm judgment, because for all we know J was in regular communication with her parents through another medium, and it is noticeable that she shows no surprise at finding herself in a materialised form holding a conversation with a living person. And the headmistresses, who were relevant to the conversation, were people with whom Denise was presumed to be in touch because of her editing work. As always in these cases you are left to choose between a simple explanation in terms of survival and a very involved explanation dispensing with it. In straightforward terms the encounter was initiated by J, the link in the story, and, after probing and prodding at other possible explanations, is the one that requires the fewest assumptions – except, of course, that survival is in itself a large assumption.

It should be said that, apart from her letter to the journal, this is the only source of Denise Iredell's important contribution to the controversial Helen Duncan literature, and it includes some material that I was given when I asked Denise to confirm the accuracy of my account, so this may be its first appearance in print. I find it difficult, as will most people, to credit the actuality of encounters with materialised dead people, but many similar incidents are reported by apparently sane people in Duncan sittings, and also with Kluski and Indridi Indridason, to name only two other notable mediums.

We come now to the third case, which was reported by Guy Lambert in the SPR Journal under the title: 'Two synchronous experiences connected with a death' (Lambert 1986). Mr Lambert made an excellent job of it, conscientiously complying with the request of the people concerned to disguise every name, place, date and identifying detail. The person reporting the experience is there called Peter Davidson, but I think he would now be prepared for me to reveal that he was the same Nigel Buckmaster whose wife had the encounter with 'Milly' at the sitting with Leslie Flint. The story has several separate threads, the main one involving Audrey, Nigel's oldest sister, and it is best to start with some general background.

Nigel had two older and two younger sisters. He was on quite close terms with three of his sisters, who, like him, were all married by that time, but Audrey, four years his senior, got married and went to live in Australia while he was still at school. She stayed in Australia for thirty years, but her marriage had broken up and she had returned to England. In 1966, when the incident I am about to relate took place, she was then fifty-one to Nigel's forty-seven. In middle-age four years age difference is negligible, but in school age children four years makes quite a gulf; and with the age difference and the long absence in Australia, Nigel felt that he hardly knew Audrey.

Their father had died two years earlier, in 1964, and Audrey, now the only unmarried sister, moved in to live with her mother, whose health had been so undermined by a thrombosis that she could not live alone. Their mother was, in fact, a very unhappy widow who had said more than once that she wanted nothing more in life than to join her husband. On 29th January 1966 she did indeed suffer another thrombosis and died. Her five children grieved at her passing but there was general agreement that this was a merciful release from suffering, so the mourning was moderated by the feeling that their mother was now at peace.

It was just forty-eight hours after their mother's death that the two synchronous incidents occurred, one to Nigel and one to Audrey. And the beautiful thing about this case is that both experiences were told to different people before either realised that they fitted together in something like a cross-correspondence.[11] It was a life changing experience for both of them. At Nigel's end, he had gone to sleep in a normal state of health and a calm state of mind. The loss of his mother grieved him, but did not agitate him, and he soon fell into a quiet sleep. But at around three in the morning he awoke suddenly, and found that

---

[11] For a revue of the early twentieth-century survival researches involving cross-correspondences see Hamilton (2017)

his heart, which had always been entirely normal, was thumping and racing in quite an alarming way. In his own words:

'I woke up in a trance-like state. I was lying on my back, conscious but immobile. I was breathing with effort and panting. I heard the beating of my heart in my eardrums. The thought came to me that this is how my mother must have felt when she had her attack and was dying. It went on for what seemed like several minutes.

Then I saw something displayed in front of me that looked like a large television screen. I felt convinced I was going to see my mother and father together, or that I was going to get some sort of a message about them in pictorial form. But that didn't happen.

Instead, to my great disappointment, all I saw was a woman's nut-brown hair appearing at the bottom right hand corner, and seeming to come out of the screen. It didn't mean anything to me. All I thought was that it was not my mother's hair, which was long, grey and straight, whereas the hair I saw was short, brown and curly.

For some reason I reached out to grasp the hair and pull it towards me, but instead of that it pulled me head first through the screen. The moment I went through the screen my heart stopped beating and I no longer had to breathe. I just floated through, and became aware that there was a golden yellow light above me.

Then I was back lying in my bed, with my heart coming to life again. It was as if my heart was being massaged back into warmth and life. Very soon I was breathing normally and was not aware of my heartbeat. I felt my heart being filled with what seemed like divine love. It was burning with love and joy – an exquisitely heavenly experience. Words cannot describe it.

I was aware of myself, and awake but with my eyes still closed; I was in a state of ecstasy and I started to have a whole series of fleeting visions, mostly scenes from my childhood days. One scene I remember vividly: I saw my four sisters and myself as young children sitting round our dining room table, but the chairs at the two ends of the table, where my mother and father would have sat, were vacant. I realised later that this was a family scene as my mother would have remembered it, and that's why it included me. At lunchtime my father would have been in his office, except on Sunday.

Another incident I saw from my mother's viewpoint related to an accident she had had three or four years earlier when she had been knocked down by a car and landed so that her head was in the gutter, facing the pavement. I saw what looked like a wall, but was actually the kerb of the pavement, and then I saw the shoes and trouser legs of a policeman walking towards me. This is what she would have seen.

At that point I opened my eyes, and then I saw a luminous cloud about eighteen inches or so above me. I hoped it was going to form into my mother's face, but it just seemed to disappear. Looking back I can see that my expectations were never realised, but that did not diminish the wonder of the experience.'

Nigel then returned to normal, or fairly normal, consciousness but found himself in a state of exaltation, with what he described as a feeling of enormous power. He went around on cloud nine for several weeks after this incident, and, though he had neither seen nor heard his mother, he had felt her presence throughout, and was now convinced of her survival, and that she was somehow 'here' and if she was here she would be in her own flat.

Pausing there, it is worth pointing out that the whole experience took place long before out-of-body and near-death experiences became well known phenomena, and it is noteworthy that though being out of body was a salient feature, he did not look down on himself from the ceiling, and the near-death element contains no tunnel. He was pulled through what looked like a giant screen, but this effected an immediate transition to the golden glow. However, the heavenly experience and sort of life review took place when he was back in his body. I say 'sort of alife review' because it was not in any way judgmental, nor were the scenes of family life seen from his viewpoint. The incidents that he remembers were all seen from the viewpoint of his mother, as if his consciousness had fused with hers, and the incident in which he found himself facing the kerb was entirely his mother's. So, in some ways, his experience was classical, or an anticipation of classical, and in other ways it is singular.

I have paused to reflect on the experience itself, but it is, in fact, just item one in a series of related incidents.

Item two is very curious indeed. Though it was soon after three in the morning when Nigel came back to what I have described as fairly normal consciousness, his behaviour then was far from normal. Without thinking too closely about what he was doing and why, he got out of bed, trying not to wake his wife, and got dressed, his intention being to go straight over to his mother's flat. (He lived at the time in Sloane Street, and his mother's flat was in Abingdon Villas, in Kensington, a mile or two distant). Audrey was, of course, still living there, but at the time it did not enter his head that Audrey had anything to do with his desire to go to the place where his mother had lived, and where her presence would be located if she was still around.

Fortunately his wife did wake up and asked what he thought he was doing, whereupon he told her his story. She pointed out that he could not go to Audrey's flat in the middle of the night, and also said that now the whole experience was fixed in their memories he should write a full account of it first thing in the morning. Under her persuasion he calmed down and went back to bed and even to sleep. His wife had learned some good habits from her acquaintance with Myers's Human Personality, which she had read many years before. The motivation for her early interest in Myers's scholarly and critical examination of survival (Myers 1901) was that her first husband had been killed on active service during the war, when they were both quite young. Though the book remained in the house, Nigel had never looked at it, and the possible post-mortem survival of his wife's first husband was understandably not much discussed .

The final and vital element rounding off this episode is the arrival next morning of Nigel's younger sister, P, at the Knightsbridge flat where she was to join with Nigel and his wife to go over to Abingdon Villas. As soon as she arrived Nigel told her the whole story. She seems to have had rather mixed feelings about the experience. She had been educated at an Ursuline convent, and, while Audrey had reacted to this schooling by becoming a militant atheist, P had become a Roman Catholic; her reaction was 'Why didn't Mummy come to me?' which, on the face of it, means that she believed that their mother had visited Nigel, though it might have implied that if her mother had really been able to visit one of her children, it would have been she herself. But what matters is that, in due course, she agreed that the whole incident had been related to her when she arrived at the Knightsbridge flat. So these three items, the experience, Nigel's subsequent compulsion to go over to Abingdon Villas, and the re-telling of the incident to P, constitute Episode one, and we now move location to Abingdon Villas for Episode two.

Audrey had been severely unsettled by her mother's death, not because she was more emotionally attached to her than was Nigel, but because she was reproaching herself bitterly for having said something that she now regretted, though it seemed quite reasonable at the time. Her mother was an invalid, and it was very comforting and convenient to have Audrey with her. But Audrey naturally enough wanted her own home again, and, a few weeks earlier, she had told her mother that they should start thinking about arrangements for a live-in companion, because she, Audrey, would like to move out. Her mother accepted this decision without protest, but, as Audrey well knew, it was a blow for her. Audrey was now tormenting herself for having upset her mother in the last weeks of her life, unnecessarily, as it had turned out. So, instead of going to bed in a fairly tranquil state of mind Audrey had been crying and working herself into a state of emotional crisis; she had taken two sleeping pills in an attempt to get some rest.

But at three in the morning she found herself woken in a very unusual way. She felt a hand grasping the hair on the back of her head. Then she heard the voice of her mother, speaking clearly and firmly, as she used to do when she was younger. The words Audrey heard were:

'Nobody need reproach themselves for anything. All my children have been wonderful.'

Audrey now wide awake, sat up in bed and called out 'Darling, where are you?' hoping that her mother would speak again, so that she could know for sure that it wasn't a dream. As if reading her thoughts, the voice spoke again, repeating the same words, but louder. Audrey was now convinced that her mother was in the room and that she would see her if she switched on the light; but when she did this there was nothing to be seen. Audrey now, like Nigel in his Knightsbridge flat, was in a state of high elation, convinced that her mother had survived and had spoken to her. She grabbed a piece of paper and a pencil and wrote down the words that she had heard.

She also wanted to tell someone about it right away, but she had to wait until morning. Her chance came when her youngest sister, J, with her Naval Commander husband, John, arrived at Abingdon Villas, fortunately well before Nigel arrived with his wife and younger sister. They found Audrey in an exultant mood, and were given a radiant account of her experience. J and John were not all that pleased to hear it, John finding it particularly embarrassing because as he saw it, a naval commander did not want to be connected with that sort of thing!

~

They did not know then that worse was to come – the arrival of Nigel with his cross-corresponding story, the incident that started with his pulling the hair of a woman he did not recognise at the time, but, when he heard Audrey's story, he realised that her hair was just like the curly, nut-brown hair of his adventure. He also realised, as a matter of further interest, that what he had interpreted as a large, flat screen, with the back of a woman's head in the lower right hand corner, was what he would have seen if he had viewed Audrey's bedroom from the window. The wall opposite the window would appear as a white rectangle, and with the bed alongside the wall Audrey's head would appear in the right hand lower corner if she was lying down facing the wall – and, of course, if he could see in the dark.

Putting the two stories together, you can construct a very plausible story. Their mother, still maintaining a presence in her Abingdon Villas flat, became aware of Audrey's distress, wanted to comfort her, but could not get through to her. Nigel was psychically much more accessible, so she took possession of him and got him to wake Audrey. When I say she took possession of him I mean part-possession, because, though he had her heart palpitations and, later, some fusion of memories, he remained himself throughout.

So J and John became key witnesses to the whole interlocking saga, because they had heard Audrey's story before Nigel and his party arrived, when they learned from Nigel's wife and sister P that they had heard his story earlier that morning. Lambert did not interview the younger sister P, and, though he talked at some length to Nigel's wife, he did not ask her for a written statement. While I regret these omissions, the fact is that J and John were the key witnesses. Lambert got signed statements from them, but only by giving an undertaking that their names would be kept strictly confidential. To the day of his death in 2006, John's nightmare was that Nigel's weird experience would become generally known, that Nigel would be identified, and that John would be contaminated by association with weirdness and subjected to ridicule. Like so many worst-case scenarios, it never happened, but I have to say that Nigel worried about his nephews and nieces (though as the offspring of Nigel's sisters, none of his relations bears his name). So when I say that J and John were reluctant witnesses I do not exaggerate.

Before looking at how the facts, as related, might be interpreted, there are some postscripts to mention. Before these episodes, Nigel had felt remote from Audrey, the age difference having been a barrier in childhood and many years absence an even greater one in later life. But Nigel had tried to bear in mind his father's expressed wish that he should look after Audrey now that she was alone. His transformative experience, as he felt it to be, had not only convinced him of survival, but he felt that he would now want to be a kinder, better person than he was before (and I have no doubt that he was in fact very nice before) and he now felt himself drawn close to Audrey, as she was to him.

There is more to come, but first I should like to take another look at the sequence of events within Nigel's own experience, because there are some puzzling features. On a literal and mechanistic view, so far as one can be mechanistic about paranormal incidents, Nigel might be said to have come out of his body, manifested in his astral form two miles west in Kensington, floated into Audrey's room by way of the window, where he saw the wall and the woman's head and materialised enough for her to feel him grasping her hair. What's definitely wrong with this story is that when he saw the wall, or the screen as he believed it to be, he was still in his body, complete with pounding heart, and did not have the out of body sensation until he went through the screen/wall – and then it was not just out of body, it was something resembling a near death experience. So how do we make sense of that? It looks as if his sighting of Audrey – assuming it was the back of her head that he saw in his vision – must have been brought about by clairvoyance or distant viewing; the distinction here being that clairvoyants and distant viewers don't have the sensation of being out of body. But how did he wake Audrey? We have to postulate something in the nature of remote psychokinesis. PK at a distance must require considerable psychic effort, so I wonder if the effort involved in the hair-pull actually precipitated the out of body experience by loosening the bonds between self and body; because it was at that moment that the out-of-body experience started and he felt himself drawn by some unseen force into the golden light.

He experienced that as being pulled through the screen, which makes slightly better sense than being pulled through the wall of Audrey's bedroom, but I should speculate that he went through the screen simply because it was there, or rather it seemed to be there, at the time he entered the out of body state. And, incidentally, though in the Journal account it sounds as if he was pulled through the screen by the head when he grasped the hair, he tells me that it was some unseen force that pulled him through, not the head .

I said there was more to come, and there is an extraordinary Episode three, which did not appear in the Journal report. Guy Lambert had asked Nigel to get in touch with him if he had any more experiences 'of that sort,' and Nigel said he would. But Nigel did not think of reporting the following incident because it was not a similar experience; but it certainly gilds an already remarkable and outsize lily.

As I said, it took Nigel a couple of weeks to come down to earth from cloud nine, and, when normal life was resumed, he thought that he ought to find out more about communication between the living and the dead. He did not start by reading Myers, but, instead, he walked down to the Spiritualist centre in Belgrave Square, and, without giving his name (which wouldn't have meant anything), he asked if he could have a session with a medium. The receptionist told him that Magdalene Kelly had just had a cancellation and directed him to her room. No sooner had he walked in and sat down when she looked up and said, in her rather broad Scots (which I shall not try to reproduce)'Oh, your mother came into the room with you – and she's asking about Nigel and Audrey.'

Nigel, a novice with beginner's luck, assumed for a long time that this is the sort of thing that you expect when you sit with a medium, and perhaps because he didn't think there was anything exceptional about this greeting he doesn't remember anything else about that sitting. But, if the rest was a nullity, it was an amazing start.

That completes the recital of facts we are given, and, if the Nigel incident and the Audrey incident were unrelated either in time or in action, they would just, each of them, have to be added to many other reports on similar lines. But the correlation and the verification by the reluctant naval commander and his wife make this a very special case. And what stands out is that it is quite difficult to explain the whole complex without invoking some input from the deceased mother.

As with every case of mental phenomena, the ultimate explanatory write-off is, of course, coincidence. There is nothing specially significant about a time pitched at forty-eight hours after a death, and twenty-four hours or seventy-two hours would do just as well. But that two people should have a seminal experience at three in the morning, both experiences centred around a deceased mother who died at this hour, seems more significant than a statistical evaluation would suggest.

When you add the link between Nigel's hand and Audrey's head, and Nigel's interesting compulsion to go to his mother's flat immediately afterwards, then these take coincidence further than I can follow it, though there is no argument one can bring to bear against anyone who prefers that explanation.

Putting chance coincidence aside, my next question is whether the two incidents – not forgetting the Magdalene Kelly postscript – can be explained without involving motivation and direction of events proceeding from the surviving mind of the mother. One must explore this possibility to the utmost, because, just as one has to prefer reasonable explanations in normal terms over paranormal explanations, one must prefer reasonable explanations in terms of human faculties over survival explanations, because we know that living people may have paranormal faculties and we don't know with equal certainty that anyone survives death.

Not knowing the full reach of the mind, let us assume that telepathy is much more active in the world than it appears to be, even though most of its influences are at a subconscious level where information that never surfaces in the conscious mind may, nevertheless, have an effect on behaviour. So, assuming very wide powers of this sort, let us suppose that Nigel knew telepathically all about Audrey's distress and self-reproach, and wanted to help her. So far as he was concerned he had no special rapport with Audrey, rather the reverse, but then he would not have been aware of all this subconscious activity.

There is, in fact, not much he can do to comfort Audrey, because the only person who can help Audrey is, in fact, her mother. So he exercises his powers of psychokinesis (of which he is equally unaware) to produce the voice of his mother to tell Audrey that all is well. The effort sends him into an out of body experience, which naturally centres on his mother, and, as Audrey can't be woken up to profit from this hallucinatory voice, he imagines waking her by psychokinetically pulling her hair. Though I have no doubt that Nigel is paranormal prone and psi conducive, and probably has more than the average degree of psychic faculty, this is a very tall order. But we must bear in mind that, however we seek to explain the correlation between Nigel's hand and Audrey's head, it looks as if remote PK is the provisional label we have to hang on it.

And though one tends to think of PK as paranormally moving things around, it must also cover moving around whatever constituents of matter have to be involved in giving Audrey the sensation of having her hair pulled. It might be that those constituents were located in her brain rather than at the back of her head, so the PK involved would amount to something like a telepathic command, or hypnosis at at a distance – but all effected without any conscious intent on the part of the agent, Nigel. As well as the hair pull, this scenario attributes to him further extraordinary capacities: first, the whole performance requires extensive powers in the nature of role-playing.

Further, he is required to have the ability not only to use some remote psychic faculty to wake Audrey, but also to cause her to hear the voice of her mother speaking a coherent sentence, and repeating it at a time when Audrey was fully awake and sitting up. That strikes me as a sustained effort going well beyond the momentary impulse required to pull the hair. If I may make a comparison: a choral singer may occasionally be required to utter a note beyond the normal range of that voice, if it is part of a fast moving sequence and can be got over quickly; but it is another thing to ask her to sing a long sustained note well out of her normal range. I should call that utterance in the voice of the mother a feat too far.

How do we fare if we start with Audrey, the one who really was in need. She wanted to hear her mother's voice, though, in fact, she never imagined that such a thing could happen. I can see a rather implausible story emerging. She determines subconsciously to hallucinate her mother's comforting words (all the more comforting because they do not imply guilt on the part of anyone) but her conscious mind, not knowing anything about this, allows her to take sleeping pills. The voice is scheduled for 3 a.m., because that is a significant time in relation to her mother. The hour arrives, and Audrey is asleep – she has failed to give herself a post-hypnotic command to wake up so that she can hear the voice. But her telepathic receptors are in better working order than her post-hypnotic powers, and she sends out a signal to Nigel, who receives the message because he is sensitive to paranormal influences, and awakes in a trance-like state in which he sees Audrey lying asleep, or at least sees the back of her head, but he does not recognise her. But subconsciously he knows that what he is required to do is use PK to wake her up by giving her the sensation of having her hair pulled. Not, to my mind, a very convincing story – in fact it reads more like a parody of a determination to dispense with a survival explanation at all costs. Crucially, I cannot see any way in which Audrey would need to involve Nigel if it was her own subconscious that was devising a plan to let her hear the voice of her mother. And Nigel was involved.

As I see it, this is one of those cases where the only person who can be seen as devising a convincing plan is the dead person. Assuming some sort of survival, one can imagine the deceased mother wanting to comfort Audrey, and to do it at a significant hour of the night, and to deliver the message direct to her. Enlisting Nigel might have been devised as a way of creating a cross-correspondence, since Nigel's action of grasping the hair makes no sense at all until it is linked with Audrey's awakening. But, as Nigel's mother was not a psychical researcher, I think it more likely that Nigel's role could have been improvised when Audrey turned out to be in a deep sleep. Starting with the mother, you get a coherent story, though that is not to say that it must be a true story. As ever, one is nowhere near certainty, but certainty is something that is always round the corner.

So these are my three cases that are difficult to explain without invoking some input from someone whose life is in the past, which is the way I tend to think of people who are dead. In each of these cases it is the dead person who is the strongest link.

THE OTHER SIDE OF THE CHANNEL

~

T he grass on the other side is not always greener, but if you want to know about its range and variety, the circumstances in which grass flourishes and conditions that may cause it to turn brown and disappear, then it is as well to look over the fence from time to time and consider your neighbour's lawn. If it looks a bit different from yours, this is something that must be of interest and importance.

It is also as well to keep actively in touch with the achievements of our predecessors. Four years from now [this was 1996] most of us and our works will be consigned to the back burner of the previous millennium, no longer current, purveyors of outdated material, and if, for example, researchers in the twenty-first century are no longer getting useful results from Ganzfeld techniques then the sort of people who today look on pre-war research as dead and gone will drop the work of present day researchers into the bottomless bin of yesterday. So let us not do likewise. The time span considered in this talk is the golden age that ran from about thirty years before the turn of the nineteenth century to some thirty years after.

'Them' in this survey refers mainly to the French, but, to a large extent, what is true of France is also true of Germany and Poland, for in all cases the leading researchers tended to be scientific in background, many of them in medicine or some branch of biology. 'Us' refers mainly to the English – under which, of course, I include the Scots and any other variety of Briton – but also to American researchers. Though times have changed, the American SPR in those days was more or less colonial, or post-colonial, and researchers like Walter Franklin Prince, a member of the clergy and a Professor of English, fit very comfortably into the mould of a typical English researcher; for, notwithstanding Sir

William Crookes, Sir William Barrett, Mrs. Eleanor Sidgwick, and later Sir Oliver Lodge, English researchers have tended to be arts grounded gentlemen, and even some ladies, very much at home in Latin and Greek. So by 'English' please understand 'Anglophone' and by 'French' include quite a lot of leading researchers in continental Europe.

The Institut Métapsychique International (IMI) came into being a generation or two later than the SPR, its notable researchers including Eugène Osty, Gustave Geley and Charles Richet; the first two were medical men; Richet was a Nobel prize-winning physiologist. They were modern professional men rather than church-respecting Victorians and Edwardians. Later came Osty's son, Marcel, and René Sudre, who, in 1956 when the golden days were over, wrote a marvellously comprehensive summary of the earlier work (Sudre 1956). Among these researchers Geley was alone in not being deeply materialist. His scientific merits must have been very widely appreciated for his speculations to have been tolerated, these including ideas that are rather difficult to distinguish from reincarnation. And if there was one thing the French could not abide it was any suggestion that they might be remotely connected with Allan Kardec and his Spiritualist followers, who enthusiastically embraced reincarnation. In fact, to be seen or heard interpreting any paranormal effect as evidence for personal survival would be to invite ridicule.

The SPR, on the contrary, right from its inception, dealt with Spiritualist mediums and their material, though applying much more critical standards than one would find in the Spiritualist movement; and while they were ever vigilant in considering alternative interpretations of the evidence, they were avowedly in pursuit of the same goal as the Spiritualist believers – they were looking for intimations of immortality.

One cannot say that the English and the French ignored one another; in the 1888 Proceedings, an article, not far short of 100 pages, by Charles Richet appeared in the original French, and Richet dedicated his monumental *Traité de Métapsychique* to William Crookes and Frederic Myers. Sir Oliver Lodge was an original committee member of the IMI, and he and Richet wrote to one another weekly and sometimes daily. So, while taking a polite interest in what was going on across the Channel, the English and the French were not so much on a collision course as on parallel tracks destined not to meet.

However, one English researcher taken very seriously by the French was Dr. W.J. Crawford, who, just after the 1914 war, published amazing reports on the physical mediumship of Kathleen Goligher and her family circle (Crawford 1919, 1919, 1921). These researches were totally ignored by the SPR, the leading English members at the time being unsympathetic to physical phenomena. Crawford, a mechanical engineer, his doctorate from Glasgow and his work based in Ulster, was decidedly not what the ruling classes of the old SPR would have considered 'one of us.'

But, on the other side of the Channel, the French were very keen on materialisation and all other aspects of mind over matter. That Crawford attributed his exceptionally obedient table movements and precisely controlled flow of ectoplasm to the co-operation of spirit "operators" was a mild irritation, a quirk of his own mythology, something to be ignored. But his weights and measures – showing how the ectoplasm supported the table by cantilevers and other mechanically plausible behaviours – that was something the French scientists could understand and appreciate.

Richet and Geley, physiologist and physician, had all the skills needed for the investigation of ectoplasm, real or supposed. Geley, writing a little later than Crawford, gave highly circumstantial descriptions (Geley 1927) of its emergence from the medium Marthe Béraud (also known as Eva C.):

> From Eva's mouth a band of white substance about two fingers' breadth slowly descends to her knees. This ribbon takes varied form under our eyes: it spreads as a large, perforated, membranous tissue, with local swellings and vacant spaces. ... I then see its end thicken, and this kind of bud expands into a perfectly modelled hand. I touch it, and it gives me the feeling of a normal hand; I feel the bones and the fingernails. Then it retreats, diminishes in size, and disappears in the end of a cord, which makes some movements and draws back into the medium's mouth.

In another extract he describes a lifesize head of a man: "I put out my hand, pass my fingers through the thick hair and feel the skull. ... An instant later everything had vanished."

Richet was just as positive in his notes dating from 1906, in the early days of Marthe's mediumship; he describes a little white mark that evolved before him into a hand with tapering fingers (Richet 1923).

> I am able to observe them very closely. I touch one of these tapers. It gives me an impression of a cold liquid. I can press on them, and I feel a bone (third phalanx), cold, covered with skin. ... Then the hand

rises and floats on the long stem that attaches it to the floor, then it falls to the floor. ... etc.

Both of them got sensational phenomena from Marthe, as did the German gynaecologist, Albert von Schrenck-Notzing (Schrenck-Notzing 1923), the same medium in his book being called Eva C., but their results pale beside those of Juliette Bisson (Bisson 1914), Marthe's friend, protector and hypnotist, who had set up a studio with the latest technology of the day with a view to obtaining photographs of materialisations, and she claims to have got a brief full form materialisation of her late husband.

However, back in England, some fairly resistant members of the SPR, who regarded all this as distasteful and almost certainly fraudulent, braced themselves to the point of organising a committee to hold a series of sittings with Marthe/Eva, to see if she could produce any phenomena under their less friendly eyes. Twenty sittings were held here in 1919 (Report 1922), and compared with her continental productions the results were scanty. The report itself discloses some inexplicable and unexplained effects, but in the end no one reached a conclusion – though they did conclude that the medium was by nature deceitful. Had she not, after all, displayed a third hand, pretending it to be her own hand resting on her knee, while her real hand played around above her head? The provenance of the third hand did not seem to concern them so much as the medium's evident duplicity. So you might say that they got what they wanted – not much. Perhaps it is significant that the report was published without anyone claiming overall authorship.

They clearly felt some embarrassment at the idea of expressing a view on the very close encounters with ectoplasm reported from over the channel; but they felt justified in standing aloof from judgment on the grounds that French researchers seldom give sufficient detail to enable others to form a judgment. There is some justification for this implied criticism, which may be a matter of national temperament. The French believe themselves to be extremely intelligent and when they say "Fraud was impossible" they expect to be taken au pied de la lettre; for to question their competence would be to imply that they are stupid: a terrible insult. They also know that their countrymen are impatient people, and, if offered a moment by moment protocol such as that offered by Everard Fielding in his report on Eusapia Palladino in 1908 (Feilding 1908) they just would not read it.

While it is true that Sir William Crookes did ask his readers to give him some credit for taking precautions, the English, on the whole, are neither surprised nor deeply offended by doubts cast on their intelligence, and it also seems that as readers, we are prepared to crawl all over these detailed protocols with the enthusiasm of detective story addicts, complaining bitterly about all the details that have been left out.

Quite apart from complaints about detail, I need hardly say that contemporary 'skeptics' attacked all these continental researchers tooth and nail, the German critics of Schrenck-Notzing being particularly virulent. But, assuming that they did not have delusions or tell lies, and that Marthe/Eva was – at least until she came to England – a materialising medium, then we have here a gradation of effects apparently dependent on the wishes and desires of the researchers. We are familiar with the experimenter effect, but the experimenter is surely tinged with the broader brush of the national preferences effect.

I slipped in "until she came to England," because three years later she completely failed to produce any effects for the investigating committee of the Sorbonne. This may sound as if it fails the nationality test, but by 'the French' I mean people engaged in psychical research; scientists of any nationality who are convinced from the start that paranormal phenomena do not exist can be expected to have a negative effect on mediumship. I also suspect that a waning Martha/Eva may never have recovered from an English committee headed by Helen Verrall, wife of W.H. Salter, long time Hon. Sec. of the SPR, who regarded materialisation as a phenomenon in very bad taste.

Going back to the dawn of psychical research in England, the objectives of the SPR, as drafted in 1882, are stated in the most poker-faced terms: it is portrayed as a sober enterprise, on a par with the collection and classification of aphids or dust-mites. The reality, as we have seen, was that some very cultivated people dedicated their spare time, of which they fortunately had a lot, to seeking evidence that had some bearing on personal survival; and, in the main, their experimental work was carried out and spontaneous material gathered in to serve this noble end, an end destined never to have an end-point.

Though the high quality of the research and writings of founding members – Frederic Myers, Edmund Gurney, philosopherHenry Sidgwick, his scientist wife (Eleanor Balfour) and other respectable academics – were universally admired, the quest for survival merited a good deal of disdain from the French. Ironically, there may be a religious basis to these attitudes. However irreligious the French, they were probably given a Catholic upbringing as small children, and this may have orientated them against disturbing the spirits of the dead. But another decisive factor is the great quantity of work done in France on hypnosis and other altered states. The work of Théodore Flournoy had a lot of influence; it was his psychic Hélène Smith (Flournoy 1900), who manifested as quite a convincing Indian princess in her trance state, and then went on to invent an elaborate but derivative language allegedly spoken on the planet Mars. Having ascertained that mediums, and the occasional multiple personality, were capable of highly consistent displays of personation and invention, the French saw no reason to consider any alternative explanations for this sort of manifestation. It was for them all role-playing.

René Sudre (Sudre, 1956), a great word inventor like all the French, objected to almost everyone else's vocabulary, and bestowed on this sort of role-play the word prosopoposis, a word that I am glad to say has not caught on. But, having once spotted that Mrs. Piper's non-French-speaking control-communicator Dr. Phinuit was a case of role-play, he considered it extremely naïve to imagine that the more plausible George Pelham or, indeed, any purported communicator could be anything more than the familiar friend prosopoposis. And it has to be said that for anyone who is not prepared to put in hours of study, some of it quite tedious, that view may seem obvious and inevitable. The French certainly saw it as a closed issue.

For example, many people would feel that a case where a Hungarian girl (Iris Farczady) – who to all appearances died but suddenly revived, now speaking only Spanish, a language she had not learned, claiming fluently and idiomatically to be Lucia[12] Altarès de Salvo, mother of 14 children - and convincing native Spaniards that she was a former citizen of Madrid – sounds like a candidate for possession or reincarnation, even though a real Lucia could not be identified (Barrington, Mulacz and Rivas 2005). But René Warcollier (Warcollier 1940-1946) readily concluded that this, too, was a manifestation of secondary personality and that the Spanish had been acquired by telepathy. I don't mean to say that because this interpretation is quintessentially French it is wrong (though the acquisition of an unrelated foreign language by telepathy strikes me as highly implausible). It just illustrates a readiness to accept unprecedented feats of telepathy rather than leaving open any hypothesis suggestive of survival.

English research also provides a lot of scope for the scythe of super-ESP, the attribution of all paranormally acquired knowledge to faculties

---

[12] Lucia' had manifested through Iris at a home séance.

of living human minds. In fact we have this paradox, that some of the strongest evidence for telepathy and/or clairvoyance comes from English sources, but of this material the most convincing evidence comes as a sidewind from researches intended to prove survival. These researches certainly prove some sort of paranormal cognition, but are not specifically designed to show what that might be. For experiments intended to distinguish between one faculty and the other, there is nothing in English research to compare with the French experiments involving Stefan Ossowiecki, Ludwig Kahn, Bert Reese, Alexis Didier (Sudre1956), and other remarkable clairvoyants, the experimenters including Geley and Richet, among others. The French were actually very lucky in having access to these exceptionally gifted psychics, who, having given their services to Paris, saw no reason to make an unpleasant sea crossing to London.

I often speculate as to what might have happened if mediums like Ossowiecki and Kluski had been handled by a typical English researcher. In France not only were they never asked to try to make contact with the deceased, they were actually discouraged. Kluski is particularly celebrated for his materialised phantoms and hands that apparently immersed themselves in molten wax leaving moulds on the table as a token of their presence; but this same medium also produced what look very much like messages from the dead. Geley (Geley 1927) describes the following event that took place one day when Kluski – in real life a poet, journalist and banker called Theodor Modrzejewski – paid a social call on Count Jules Potocki, also a member of the IMI, on 22nd November, 1920 (pp. 261-3).

The conversation started with politics then moved to mediumship, whereupon Kluski asked for pencil and paper, and, in a light trance, wrote down a conversation in two distinct handwritings, ostensibly between two of Potocki's deceased friends, who appeared to be deeply confused at finding Potocki in their presence, correctly believing him to be still living. They discuss how he has aged, and wonder who the other man is, i.e. the medium. They express astonishment that when Potocki touches Kluski they find themselves touched; they say that after this Potocki could not possibly doubt survival but, in case he does, they offer him evidence of identity by bringing his deceased brother, Thomas, who immediately reminds him of some intimate, wholly private conversation they once had.

It is surprising that Kluski was prepared to make these religiously forbidden excursions into the realms of the supposedly sleeping dead, but perhaps he did not feel responsible for the writings of his hand. In England or America he would surely have been pressed into service as an other-world communicating medium, but Geley, though awestruck by Kluski's automatic writing, asked him to refrain from it while he was in Paris, because it reduced the potency of his physical effects. Geley was, perhaps, justified in feeling that the production of wax-moulds was more crucial, in that it resulted in a permanent product, but he also knew what was wanted by the scientific membership of the IMI. What was not wanted was a display of mind-reading+role-playing purported messages from 'beyond.'

Just as the IMI researchers preferred to leave survival to what they called 'the spiritists' there is an important area of research that the English left almost entirely to the French, i.e. experimentation in the field of precognition. The English evidence for precognition rests on well-researched spontaneous cases, such as the collection put together by Eleanor Sidgwick in 1888 (Sidgwick 1888). This may be something to do with the law, which in England has acted vigorously against fortune-tellers. The High Court pronounced early in the century that as it was impossible to tell the future, anyone purporting to do so for reward must ipso facto be perpetrating a fraud. Perhaps the French law is more indulgent, because fortune telling is just what Osty's clairvoyants were doing before, during and after the 1914 war, and so far as I know, England has seen nothing like it.

Osty himself had the personal experience (Osty 1922) of asking a clairvoyant where and when he would find a suitable dwelling in Paris, and was given the answer in specific and entirely correct detail. The property, with its predicted covered path leading to the entrance and statue in front, was acquired by a sequence of chance events unconnected either with the medium and or with any steps taken by Osty. He called it the best lesson in philosophy that he had ever had, and he went on to record equally accurate predictions made by his professional mediums Jeanne Morel and Raoul de Vallière (Osty 1923).

Most of his sitters, being practical people, did not set puzzles just for the pleasure of unsettling notions of causality. They asked about their business enterprises, or where they would be posted on war service, and what they should do to better themselves. Osty's material was so copious that he was able to draw one firm conclusion from it: every person, according to his theory, has within him knowledge of his own past and his own future, and this is what the medium can read. On this view, there is no such thing as reading the future except as it affects the individual inquirer. Apart from some rumours of good advice given on Brighton pier, there is no comparable body of research finding here. Or if there is – and one always has to guard against there being black holes loaded with material of which one is entirely ignorant – then it is not as commonly known as it should be. With our sights so firmly set on the next world, English sitters and experimental researchers have not been nearly so curious about next week.

The French precognition researchers were actually observing experiments involving the use of psychometry, and, while there does not seem to have been any programme specifically aimed at investigating the technique of using an article as a link to a person or place, the accumulated reports provide a substantial body of material on which to theorise. The use of psychometric objects has been endemic in the testing of mediumship, and, in the very early days, well before the founding of the SPR, a vast amount of work was done on psychometry in America by Joseph Buchanan and William Denton (Denton 1988), though their main purpose was usually to get a description of the environment from which the object was taken.

Clairvoyants such as Ossowiecki seem nearly always to have based their readings on psychometric objects, though, when the purpose of a test was for him to give a psychic reading of the words or drawing inscribed on a sheet of paper inside an envelope, the test is usually classified as an exercise in clairvoyance rather than one in psychometry. In fact, Ossowiecki always went well beyond the task of describing the target, and launched into character and life descriptions of the person who supplied it; and this is what is usually understood as psychometry. It is often treated as a faculty on par with clairvoyance, but I see it as a technique facilitating clairvoyance by clearly identifying the target person or place.

Quite apart from the precognitive aspect, there is no body of research in English in this century to compare with Osty's vast collection of reports on his psychometrists, with one exception, viz. the work of Gustav Pagenstecher, a German who settled in Mexico, and whose lengthy reports (Pagenstecher 1923), were also published in the Proceedings of the ASPR for 1922. This was due to the active co-operation of Walter Franklin Prince, who visited Mexico specifically to meet Pagenstecher, and to take part in some of the experiments – unfortunately, the less successful ones.

What is so fascinating about Pagenstecher is that he was experimenting at the same time as Osty (though Osty was extremely active on all fronts both before and after Pagenstecher), and both of them got such dramatic results that they were able to extract principles and draw up something like the laws of psychometry. But they did not know about each other, and, sad to say, Osty's laws of psychometry based on his data, derived from a number of professional mediums (whom he considered the best subjects) are quite different from those of Pagenstecher, based on his researches with just one talented amateur, whose gift was discovered accidentally.

To take a few examples, Osty noted that if half a dozen people had handled the link object the medium would refer first to the last person to handle it; Osty would usually then say "No, go back further," and might get a description of the person who gave it to him. Told to go back to the person before that, the medium would finally arrive at the target person (All of which, by the way, shows how a determination to keep silent and unhelpful may cause such an experiment to fail).

It was quite otherwise with Pagenstecher's psychometrist, Senora Z (for Zierold), a married woman who freely gave her services for research. If anything dramatic had happened in the presence of the object – and the more calamitous the better – she would focus immediately on that incident. If she did not find herself swept into some catastrophe at which (unlike Osty's psychometrists) she would feel herself to be personally present, drowning, choking or whatever, then she went back, not to the people who most recently held, touched or owned the object, but to the people who originally manufactured it, and she would find herself in a paper factory; or she would by-pass the manufacture and go straight back to the ultimate origin, a tree in its natural state before it was turned into pieces of paper.

Osty's version has a degree of scientific plausibility if one imagines people's DNA coating the object in layers that have to be penetrated by the psychic feelers; Pagenstecher's makes more sense if one makes the leap that Pagenstecher rather surprisingly made from atheist-materialist to survivalist-spiritualist, believing firmly that the spirits of the dead came to display their crises to the entranced Senora Z. On this hypothesis, the link object can be seen operating as a sort of mobile phone summoning the person whose number is in its store. However, no thesis is entirely consistent: Pagenstecher certainly believed that objects had to be touched by the person concerned and were also impregnated by their environment, whereas Osty pointed out that once a psychometrist had made contact with the target person, she could continue to derive information after the object had been destroyed and she could paranormally cognise events that had taken place after the object left the presence of the person, even after that person had died.

Needless to say, information derived from what Osty described as a 'completed life' presented him with an embarrassing problem, because he assumed that once contact was made with the target person via the link object, the psychometrist derived most of her information by telepathy. But, in the case of a completed life, from whose mind? In one of his cases an aged servant disappeared from an estate, and a scarf of his, taken from his cupboard, was given to the psychometrist. She pronounced, as no English medium would have expressed herself, that the person did not exist any more. Nevertheless, she was able to describe how he had left the house, the route he had taken, the left or right turns that had led him to the place where he had collapsed, information that proved to be correct but was unknown to any living person. Osty's preferred solution is in rather imprecise terms of retrocognitive telepathy.

Another practical theme in French literature is the use of metagnomy (Osty's preferred word for psi activity of whatever description) for trailing criminals from the scene of the crime even to their lair (Osty 1927). Ossowiecki was called on more than once to assist police in pursuit of criminals, but he operated by retrocognitive clairvoyance. The English may talk of a sixth sense, and there are supporters of the limbic system, the hippocampus and the pineal gland, but the quintessentially English concept of the psychic faculty is an etheric apparatus floating somewhere behind the eyes – the ghost in the machine. Can one see an English medium on the physical trail, like a human bloodhound? Not really. For tracking you need people who conceive of psi in more biological terms as being in some ways analogous to a scent.

For the greatest contrast between French and English experience we have to go back again to Myers, not this time directly on the search for immortality but in his intense fascination with hypnosis and the trance state. This was, in fact, a necessary preliminary to the greater quest; for a man dedicated to contemplating survival of human personality the first question must be to have a clear idea of what is meant by personality, and hypnosis has the most disturbing implications, especially if it resulted in dissociation. If a new personality sub-division can be called forth by hypnosis, who is the real you? If memories can be put into your mind so that you can't distinguish the pseudo-memory from your own real memories, then how does memory define your personality? If a post-hypnotic command can compel you to carry out an action and to invent a plausible reason to justify the action, then who is the person you believe to be responsible for your own decisions, the 'you' who is making a bid to survive? (Myers 1885).

The early English hypnotists like Esdaile certainly reported some sensational effects, such as the 'mesmerising' of water which, when later consumed by a patient, could send him into a hypnotic state or make him sleep. But when Myers wrote his massive articles on hypnosis for the SPR Proceedings, he had to rely on French experimental work, and, on the occasions when he was personally present, together with his physician brother, he was a participating guest and observer rather than a co-experimenter (Myers 1886).

Myers was probably the first English researcher to observe that what happens in France would not necessarily happen in England (or so he hoped). He was referring, in particular, to a rather alarming incident in which a good hypnotic subject had the idea fed to her that she had a powerful grudge against a magistrate, and when a searing hatred had been built up she was handed a firearm, told it was loaded, and invited to shoot the supposed magistrate, which she proceeded to do with great enthusiasm. Myers, trying to remain as polite as possible in the circumstances, says that he would not expect such a display of violence from his less volatile compatriots!

But the most crucial testimony from France came in reports clearly demonstrating the effects of telepathic hypnotic command. The most well known of these commands given at distance were the experiments of Pierre Janet; but he was not alone, for, in some later tests, personally witnessed by Myers, another French hypnotist was able to entrance a woman servant at randomly selected times of the day and get her to carry out specified actions. What treasures might flow into the coffers of psychical research if any hypnotist today could show that he could give commands at a distance – except that today it would be assumed that some form of technology was at work enabling the hypnotist to trigger the action. The question is academic, because no English hypnotist appears to have made such a claim, and even in France this seems to have been a short-lived phenomenon. Perhaps it died out because people lost confidence in it.

An even more short-lived effect is included in René Sudre's very comprehensive treatise, though most people would regard it as an unfortunate episode in physical chemistry rather than in psychical research; this is the announcement in 1903 by Prof. Blondlot of Nancy that he had discovered radiation emitted by metals in a certain state of molecular equilibrium (Sudre 1960). He studied his N-rays, calculated their wavelength and described their action on phosphorescent bodies. Another French researcher found N-rays emitted in muscular and nervous activity. But no one outside France ever found any N-rays, and, pretty soon, no one in France found them any more. It was agreed that N-rays did not exist, and the unfortunate Blondlot was discredited, which is sad because, if he had been a member of the IMI, it might have occurred to him that he found N-rays because they had been created for the nonce by the force of his imagination and belief.

For this is the conclusion to which this revue of Anglo-French relations has led: not only do researchers determine the sort of effects that will show up in their experiments, but peoples and nations have a hand in it too. Wishful thinking is, I suggest, much more productive than it is generally reckoned to be. When people feel very confident about their goals and their means, and they feel confident about themselves and their society, then they generate material that responds to their desires and expectations.

The founders of the SPR aimed very high; you could not aim higher than to try to make a bridge between the living and the dead. It is difficult to imagine what would be required for the enterprise to be generally accepted as having succeeded, and, in the absence of clear success, one has to settle for the fuzzy logic of 'not proven' – a verdict that leaves all issues open. But the straightforward opposite of success is failure, and the repercussions of failure have, I suspect, cast a cloud of insecurity over English research in this area. In America, Rhine, in the 1930s, sent American research (and academic research world wide) off on a completely new course, highly successful for many years, though mostly in the land of its conception and birth. It, too, has so far failed in its relatively modest aim of identifying personality types and other factors enabling people to be selected and conditions to be determined that would lead to reliable demonstrations of psi by groups of people who are not exceptionally psi-gifted.

The French were, from the start, on to something more earthbound, more practical, viz the examination and classification of the various forms of paranormal cognition and the exercise of mind over matter. These objectives were closer to the real world of science, and could be regarded as an attempt to extend the boundaries of biology. In these enterprises they were extremely successful, and the years from the First World War to the 1930s were really a golden age of fruitful experimentation. After 1940 the nation was demoralised, and, so far as I know, that spirit of glad confidence has not re-emerged, and in Europe, generally, science is believed (especially by those defending fairly modest scientific positions) to exclude all possibility of paranormal action.

As to what will happen to psychical research in England, who can say? But I think it lies in our hands, or the hands of our successors, because the moral I draw from the comparison between these two cultures is that the paranormal does not just happen to us entirely by chance: it happens because we make it happen.

PART FOUR:

WIDER ANGLES AT GREATER LENGTH

INTRODUCTION

~

These articles all deal with issues fundamental to psychical research, the first tackling the basic question of how rational people can be justified in having a high degree of confidence in the reality of paranormal phenomena when psi cannot be demonstrated to order, and, when psi could (it is claimed) be demonstrated to order, it was by individuals or groups to whom only a limited number of interested people could have access, few of whom would have had control over conditions. Add to that the fact that there have been many fraudsters in the field (most of the exposures having been made by researchers) and the confident assurances by the scientist-in-the-street, and his spokesman journalist, that psi is impossible because it infringes 'the laws of science,' and the question of authenticity becomes a major concern. The article on proof, written in 1990 (revised in 2003), deals with these issues.

Jott is a relative newcomer on the psychical research agenda, and has until very recently made its appearance only in SPR and related publications (see Jinks 2016 and Barrington 2018). Of all phenomena, jott is the easiest to dismiss as entirely due to normal human failings, but there is good reason to accept a core of incidents as authentic, in which case this marginal phenomenon has large implications. This chapter focuses on the case material, but also seeks to reconcile the extreme effects of environmental breakdown with the norms of day to day existence. The relationship of jott to the maintenance of a stable reality figures significantly in subsequent chapters.

The ambitiously titled small theory gathers various psi material together and comes to some conclusions extending rather beyond the confines of psychical research. The original lecture was condensed from a more extensive survey of the field, and the compression sometimes makes for propositions not as amply supported as they could be.

The final chapter, on psychic force, tries to draw threads together and continues attempts made in the previous articles to relate psi effects to the causal system in which we are embedded, that is to say, normal life.

PROOF – THE VALIDATION OF SINGULAR EVENTS

~

What is proof? And what is reality? I am reminded of the unfortunate foreigner with an imperfect grasp of English usage of the definite article who inquired of a stranger "Vat is time?" Unfortunately for him he happened upon a philosopher rather than a policeman, and the philosopher, stroking his beard, said 'Sir, you have asked a very profound question.' That is rather the way I have come to feel about proof. If you ask a difficult question you get a difficult answer.

It was in connection with psychical research that I first asked this question, because paranormal phenomena distinguish themselves from most other forms of experience by being sporadic, unreliable, unpredictable, unrepeatable, demonstrable only by one or two people in every generation, if that, and by normal standards a-causal; and, of course, impossible. So how do we prove that paranormal incidents have reality? In the light of this problem I asked the question.

I started by taking down a book called *Philosophy made Simple*, which is how it has to be if I am going to understand it. To my great dismay PROOF was not indexed. But if you regard something as proved, or proven, if you prefer, you are (I think) making a statement about your state of knowledge, and Philosophy made Simple reminded me that Hume – David, not Daniel – brought philosophy to a lurching halt by proving that you cannot know anything. This is called the problem of knowledge. After that, scientists took over from the philosophers, and scientists do not have that problem (nor, come to that, do lawyers). But scientists have their own problem, a variety of the Jowett syndrome:

I am the Master of this College;
What I don't know isn't knowledge.

What scientists tend to assert is that nothing can be regarded as known unless it is susceptible to scientific modes of proof, and has been shown to be established by those methods. 'Known' is equated with scientifically proven. That is surely a great mistake, because most things that actually happen in the world, or are supposed to happen, are not open to scientific investigation, and yet they are real events. Tomorrow no one will be able to prove scientifically that today's events took place, but would you consider yourself to be lacking in scientific rigour if you were, here and now, convinced that yesterday you woke up, had breakfast, etc. There must be ways of knowing, and being sure, other than by scientific proof; otherwise we wouldn't know much.

At this point please imagine a diamond shaped diagram. Sitting there aloft, nearest to heaven and furthest from the ground, you see the words 'Mathematical proof': that is to say, proof by incontestable logic. Once you have learned the lesson of Pythagoras and his theorem you can sit back and be one hundred percent sure that the square on the hypotenuse really does equal the sum of the squares on the other two sides. You have an absolute proof, and therefore absolute certainty. And note that we are not talking about any particular triangle that existed in the past, or that will exist in the future. We are really talking about a platonic idea of a right-angled triangle, something detached from the specifics of time and place.

I gather that mathematicians, happy at last with a proof of Fermat's last theorem, still have to suffer uncertainty when it comes to Goldbach's conjecture – a proposition that even I can understand: that all even numbers can be broken down into two prime numbers. It seems that computers can furnish umpteen examples to illustrate this great truth, but trial and error is not the same thing as proof in the first degree, because that tells you exactly why, even if it takes a few hundred pages of argument.

Sometimes the proof seems to arrive before anyone knows that there is anything to prove. Among anecdotes that I once picked up on Open University TV is the feat performed by the nineteenth century Irish mathematician, William Hamilton. He proved that if you had a prism with bi-axial symmetry, which he did not have, then light focused on the surface would pass through as a single ray but emerge from the other side in conical form, whereas light striking at another angle would break up to form a hollow cone and emerge the other side as a hollow cylinder. He was later proved to be right when the requisite prism came to hand. But which was the proof? If two groups working with different prisms came up with conflicting results then mathematics, the supreme manifestation of truth, would prove that one lot had got it right and the other lot had not. But supposing everyone working with a bi-axially symmetrical prism found no signs of a cone or hollow cylinder, then who would you believe? That the prism experts were wrong, that the experimenters were wrong or that the mathematical proof was wrong? In the real world, removed from on high, proof would not always win the day.

Outside mathematics – and most of personal life does seem to carry on without any mathematical counterpart – there are explanations and partial explanations that look rather like equations. My chemistry book tells me that if you put an iron nail into copper sulphate solution the result will be a nail coated with copper and a green liquid where before you had a blue liquid. I suppose this must have been a fairly reliable sequence of events long before anyone had the slightest idea why this might be so.

Comes the day when someone can write on the board $Fe + CuSO_4 = FeSO_4 + Cu$, and that looks very similar to some simple equation like $(a+b)^2 = a^2+2ab+b^2$, but, despite the similarity, these two explanations are not quite *in pari materia*. The chemical equation is a mere description of what is happening, that the iron is pushing the copper out of the solution, and, in terms of chemistry, it is a very partial explanation, one that would be amplified, in the course of time, by further explanations in terms of atomic structure and core charge and I know not what (and had better not try to say).

The point is that before any of the explanations, people who put nails into copper sulphate would have been in no doubt as to what was going to happen and what did happen. They were convinced because it happened and they would have considered it a demonstrable fact of science though there was no theory to back it up. And, on the basis of past experience, they could predict future events.

An explanation is a lovely thing, and one can see why scientists find it so satisfying. My brief acquaintance with chemistry was very short on explanation. I knew that salt dissolved in water and even understood that the components separated into ions. I was thrilled, years later, to see a new school textbook with marvellous illustrations showing the break up of sodium chloride, two water molecules heading towards the positive sodium, negative oxygen leading the way like two red-nosed policemen, green negative chlorine surrounded by pale but positive hydrogen prongs protruding from an asymmetrical water molecule; here, I felt, was something entirely convincing, something that didn't just happen, but something that had to happen. Without actually seeing any of this take place, you feel that when an explanation hangs together so perfectly, it has to be right.

John Stuart Mill thought that the then-emergent atomic theories might transform chemistry from an inductive science, reliant on observation and experiment, into a deductive science where the scientist just thinks and reasons. I think he was saying, or implying, that this would raise it to a status close to the mathematically exact. But it can never get there. In school geometry there would seem to be no way Pythagoras could be unseated, but, in applied science, theories can indeed prove to be wrong or faulty, however well they seem to fit the facts.

As an example of faulty theory, the great eighteenth century chemist Lavoisier classified heat as an element, so that a body was hot because it contained heat. But, regardless of why, things got hot when they were heated. The demonstrable proof that salt dissolves in water is really to show that it does. The supporting explanation adds weight. There is always room for weight, because, outside maths, there is no such thing as 100% certainty. Strictly speaking, 'proof' should be eliminated from popular speech, but that means losing a short and useful word; it should, however, be understood to have quotation marks around it. What is beginning to show a nose above the water is that a scientifically proved principle and a real effect are not necessarily identical.

The weight added to a demonstration is rather like the weight added by motive to a sequence of objective clues. The detective finds that the supposed murderer has been identified as leaving the scene: his fingerprints are there, the victim's blood is on his clothes, but there is no shred of motive. This leaves a big hole in the detective's case and in his sense of certainty. Now he finds the motive and it all hangs together. Motive is a very probative factor, but standing alone it proves nothing.

You can put salt into water any day of the week, but there are many established facts of nature that you cannot demonstrate except by waiting for them to happen. Some of them happen with frequency and regularity. In pre-scientific times, as now, the sun (presumably) rose on one side of the horizon and sank on the other. The tides came and went. People may have theorised that the regularity of the heavens were arranged by the gods to assist astrologers and sundials, and they may have thought that Thor was gathering up the waters to take a bath, but, however wrong they were about the explanations, could they have doubted that sunrise and high tide were proven facts of nature?

Certainty, the fact that high tide would happen about six hours after low tide rested entirely on past performance and the ability to predict on the basis of regular observation. Proof, in the sense of being able to show that your prediction was correct, would have to wait upon the event, and is really better described as validation of a prediction. But, as you stood on a dry beach looking out on a barely visible strip of sea at midday, you would surely be entitled to tell a sceptical visitor from a Mediterranean country that, within six hours, the Atlantic waters would be raging over your heads if you stayed where you were.

Would or should your certainty about this cycle of events be any more securely based because you know, or more probably have a very vague idea, that tides are something to do with the gravitational pull of sun and moon? If regular natural events are reliable to the point of invariability, an explanation adds very little weight to the certainty that you are entitled to feel about a frequently verifiable event. Whether or not you understand what is meant by gravitation – and it seems that those who do are in acrimonious disagreement with one another – you do not doubt the reality of alternating tides or falling apples.

So far all the events considered here have been predictable, either because they happen with ordered regularity or can be made to do so, and repeated observations enable you to enunciate a principle to the effect that they can, do and will take place. Demonstration and Prediction can now be placed to left and right of the diamond, so that they form a triangular pediment with mathematical proof sitting aloft on its own. As I said, mathematical propositions are timeless and placeless, but Demonstration and Prediction are concerned with events in the real world that are to take place at a definite time in the future; in a demonstration someone has arranged things so that the event will take place as a result of these arrangements, and in a prediction the predictor has identified the conditions that will lead to the predicted event.

But we have not finished with reality yet – in fact, we have hardly started. Life as we know it consists almost entirely of apparently random happenings, just one thing after another, but some of nature's surprises may, in time, move into the predictable class when more is known about them. Eclipses have moved up a class, so to speak, but tidal waves and earthquakes still take people by surprise. A tidal wave, or tsunami, was reported in Hawai a few years ago, but, speaking for myself, I have never seen a tidal wave, and have never seen Hawai, come to that. Tidal waves do not seem to happen round the coast of Britain, so how do I know that they happen at all? How would you set about proving to me that they do happen? This is where tidal waves differ from dissolving salt and falling apples. The only way we can know that they can happen is to become convinced by evidence that tidal waves have happened, and to be sure of that you must be sure that a particular earthquake, here and there, did happen. So the answer to the original question depends on information gained from identifiable past events.

You could explain various theories on what is thought to cause tidal waves, and that might sound plausible, but I am not well informed enough to know whether your explanation is good science. You certainly can't arrange for one to take place. I am not much better off than if you told me that they happened because God was angry with the wicked, and nobody knew what would set him off. So why should I accept that tidal waves happen? And, if I do, on what basis do I accept it? On the basis, I have to say, of the rankest hearsay; but then hearsay can be entirely veracious. Tidal waves, I tell myself, are talked about in serious books as if they were a recognised class of geophysical event. Several have been reported recently in high quality newspapers. I can think of no plausible reason for these stories' being invented, and I should think there would be an enormous international outcry if news media reporters faked shocking tragedies and got people to subscribe to imaginary funds. I have actually seen on television what have purported to be people fleeing from tidal waves – though they might have been pure fiction – and heard people tell their dramatic stories.

This is just the sort of evidence we have to rely on to be sure that tidal waves actually happen, and, when all things are considered, the evidence for the existence of tidal waves is somewhat less copious than evidence for the existence of poltergeists. All in all, is the case for tidal waves, and for Poltergeists, proved? Can we speak here of proof? It is more a case of Verification, being satisfied or convinced by the testimony. I do not actually find myself significantly less sure about the reality of tidal waves, which I have not witnessed, than I am about high and low tide, which I have. So I reckon that when you're sure, you're sure – anything above 99% sure will do, and the fact that you might add a few .999s onto your sureness about the sunrise, tides or earthquakes does not make all that much difference.

But, beyond the sunrise, tides and earthquakes are those singular events that fall into no familiar framework or context, because they are unexpected, unlikely, and sometimes one-off events. Selecting one at random, what about thousands of jellyfish that arrived a few years ago in the North Sea and blocked the water intake of a power station, a startlingly improbable event that, with any luck, may never happen again. How would you satisfy yourself that it ever happened at all?

It is clear enough that you cannot prove it by laying on a demonstration, and, unless you have the sort of gifts we are always looking for, you cannot make a prediction to say when it will happen again, though you might say, in a general way, that if the climate gets warmer we may expect to find some very obnoxious marine life in northern waters. You also have to say, against its veridical status, that jellyfish blocking of cooling inlets is not something that you commonly read about in serious books. It was just a specific thing that happened, or is claimed to have happened, and you want to be satisfied that it was a real event, as real as the salt in the sea, and not just a sensational story made up by the media.

Psychical researchers will recognise this problem and know how to go about tackling it. First I refer to my source of information, which is, again, The Times itself. But if you did not read about it you are hearing about it from me, so you have more questions to ask about it than I have; you have to consider how likely it is that I have invented the whole story. An explanation was forthcoming at the time, and it sounded convincing.

I argue that The Times is usually reliable as a source of information, and, though you shouldn't believe everything you read in the newspapers, they are not likely to have published a report about a named power station if the story had been substantially untrue; perhaps the size of the jellyfish might have been exaggerated by a small margin, but jellyfish there must surely have been. If it had been a complete invention, there would have been an indignant rebuttal from the director of the power station, leading to retraction and even apology from The Times. That is good enough for my purposes, but if my whole view of life depended on it I should make further inquiries – look up the back numbers of The Times, find the name of the power station, write to the director, question employees, examine the site, seek out expert opinion, ask around in the neighbourhood, speak to the reporter, and (crucially) assess all the witnesses as purveyors of truth. Then I might finally be satisfied.

And, when I am satisfied, how satisfied am I entitled to be? Am I sure that this unusual event happened? If my expressing or holding a false view of its ontological status would result in my being sent to serve a term of life imprisonment in Saudi Arabia, or spend ten years in the salt mines of Siberia, or even in our own salubrious open prison, I should certainly say 'Yes, it happened.' The Siberia test, as I term it, is a wonderful way of focusing the mind on how reasonable it is, and how likely to be right, for one to adopt a Humean scepticism in the assessment of evidence. The Siberia test forces a decision on a balance of probabilities, which might be a mere 51:49, not a very high standard. I am, in fact, more certain than that. I am sure beyond reasonable doubt, a standard closer to 99:1. However, it is clear enough that my certainty has nothing to do with scientific proof. There may once have been jellied remains to be seen at the site, but I should have to take someone else's word for it that they were there.

We approach the awesome truth, which is that most facts in life are 'proven' by the methods I have outlined, which are the methods of the historian, the lawyer, the policeman and any other rational person who wants to know what has actually happened – not what can happen under certain circumstances, not what will happen on defined occasions, but what did happen. This is how you 'prove' that the Thames used to freeze over at times in the seventeenth century so that horses and carriages could cross it and people could hold fairs on it. This is how you prove that the Queen's Hall, the principal venue for orchestral concerts, was demolished by a bomb in the 1940s. It is also how you prove that filing cabinets, chandeliers and pictures moved about of their own volition in a lawyer's office in Rosenheim and that the misbehaviour of the office telephone system baffled scientists from the Max Planck Institute.[13] But it is not only in psychical research that the reality of events has to be proved by these methods. This is also the way you prove that Eddington and his team, testing the veracity of Einstein's theories on gravity, took some rather blurry photographs that demonstrated the bending of light in a gravitational field. We must (remembering Siberia) take or leave their word for it that their photographs were taken in the location they describe and not mocked up elsewhere.

It is true that science, which tells you what can happen, and seeks to tell you why, aims to move on beyond historical fact. Its business

---

[13] One of the best attested and sensational poltergeist cases took place in German village of Rosenheim in 1967 (Bender 1967).

is to re-enact the event using improved technology, verify the cause and enunciate the principle. Rutherford's demonstration of particles passing through atoms does not have to be verified by reference to his personal experiments, because other scientists can demonstrate the effect. But let us note that the quest for a principle has to be grounded on data from reports of past events, events that have to be evaluated in just the same way as those displays of paranormality at Rosenheim.

Scientists do not usually generate their own data personally, because no one can be an expert in every field; so scientific inquiry starts with reliance what other people say. Once a principle has been propounded it is, again, only experts in the field who will be able to verify it – others have to depend on them and assess their reliability. Each verification in turn becomes a past event, and other people have to rely on it as a report. So, to navigate reality, we are all dependent on evaluation of things that are said to have happened. The verification of past events is not achieved by considering whether they ought to have happened according to rules, regularities or principles, but by inquisition, which is directed at discovering whether they did in fact happen. Inquisition is a tedious process, and you never reach the end of your inquiries, though you can reach a vanishing point, the point of satisfaction. Can you ever be as satisfied as you are about Pythagoras? In theory, no, but then remember that there are very convincing ways of showing that 1=2, and, if you cannot spot the fallacy in the argument, you might do better to feel sure that there really was a hurricane here in England in 1987, or that you did indeed listen to the radio news this morning, though that event has now passed into history, beyond the reach of science.

Back to earthquakes and other things that never happen to most of us. Some readers may be bursting to point out that earthquakes do in fact leave objective traces behind so that archaeologists can bring scientific certainty to the hearsay of history. That is true, and it leads me to point out that the sort of past events I have mentioned so far belong to the world of things. But non-geographical events also belong in the web of history and have reality. When you bring in behaviour, problems of proof proliferate, and the paranormal does appear to be a behavioural phenomenon. Even the most physical paranormalities are not ordinary anomalies such as belong in the realms of unsolved science; psychic anomalies appear to be related to will, mood and personality.

So I am on the way to bringing in the paranormal, but first I think a short recapitulation is in order, and I shall return to the invisible visual aid, which has mathematical proof sitting at the top with Demonstration on the left and Validation on the right. Inquisition may now be placed at the lower extremity of the diamond, and the visual aid is now complete. However, these terse descriptions can do with some amplification. Ignoring mathematical proof, the three classes stand as follows:

1. Demonstration: The ascertainment of a replicable and reliable effect; and demonstrating the effect necessarily entails sufficient understanding of its cause.

2. Validation: The ascertainment of a recurrent and predictable effect; and predicting the effect may or may not entail understanding of its cause.

3. Inquisition: The verification of an occasional or singular event, regardless of any causal context that may be attributed to it.

This is the historical mode of fact finding. It includes personal observation, the testimony of personal observers, the testimony of more remote informants and any objective exhibits from which deductions can be made.

It will be seen that Class 3 covers a range of incidents, from occasional to singular. An occasional event is an activity of a recognised type known to occur from time to time, while a singular event is *sui generis*, in a class of its own, a one-off surprise. But, just as an unpredictable event can move up a class and become a predictable effect with a recognisable cause, so may a singular event turn out to be occasional rather than singular.

Scientists in general don't have to deal with events that seem to have no cause, because the paranormal lies outside the usual scope of science. Those scientists who do study it have rather limited scope for strictly scientific methodology, and are frequently assailed by the ultimate insult that what they are doing is not science. But, as we have seen, scientists dealing with normal events also have to depend on historical modes: in other words they have to make the best of observation, evidence and testimony.

Personal observation necessarily plays a very limited role, since the observer cannot be everywhere observing everything, nor is an observer equipped to make reliable observations in specialities outside his own. And, unpalatable though it may be to the scientific spirit, the status of all events not personally and efficiently observed relies ultimately on testimony. The very laws of science, such as they are believed to be at any time, rest on the testimony of other people, and, so long as they report events that fit in with the current paradigms, those witnesses are believed, and believed in just the same way, and for the same reasons, as providers of historical source material. Most people know next to nothing about the laws of science, but feel that there is great strength in the ability of scientists to check up on one another by replicating any effect for which they feel some doubt. Well, a team of scientists are reported to have descended into the bowels of the earth, somewhere in Europe, to try to register a blip that just might happen this year or next year, their purpose being to prove that most of the matter in the universe is invisible. Try replicating that.

I should now like to move on from the domain of physical events that just happen, and deal with incidents that are brought about by volition or at least by behaviour. We are now well out of the mainly mineral-vegetable world and into the mainly animal world, so much more complicated. What are the routes to certainty here?

Demonstration.

Can anything be demonstrated about people? Biology is not all that different from chemistry, so that, clearly, you can seize anyone in the street and show that his heart is beating. But can you say with scientific certainty that because he is wearing a cloth cap he will definitely vote left? Obviously not. You may have picked on a lifelong Tory worker or a titled country gentleman on a day out in town. Once mind and will enters the picture you can forget about geography, chemistry and biology. We are into psychology. The defence mechanism test (DMT) can, it is claimed, be applied with a high degree of confidence that the result will be a reliable indicator of the behavioural tendency known as defence mechanism. This is, apparently, something about people that can be demonstrated, but still no one claims that it will yield an expected result every time without fail. Perhaps it will work out with 70%, 80% even 90% reliability. That is not certainty, but psychology is recognised as a science, so it seems that statistical degrees of certainty are acceptable as proof of an objective effect. But your demonstration is reliable only on a probabilistic basis.

Validation.

This concerns effects that can be predicted because they have a degree of recurrence in their character. Predictions are certainly made about behaviour but, again, only in terms of statistical certainty. Insurance companies remain in business because they know roughly how many people will set their houses on fire, crash their cars or die just when they are about to draw their pension. Students of the Poisson distribution were able to calculate, presumably in pre-war days, how many years were due to go by before it was time for a horse to kick a Prussian army officer to death – and the horse seemed to know, too. It is all scientific methodology, just like the theory that tells you how long it will take for half the radiation in a radioactive substance to break free, though no one can say which particle will go and which will stay.

At this point we can say a few more words about the paranormal. It does seem that demonstration based on the supposed talents of the average person, or the average student, could lead to statistical certainty. It may well be that, in the normal way, if one can put it like that, powers of ESP and PK are so thinly distributed that we have to be treated as amounting to a swarm of particles, insubstantial as individuals but sturdy taken en masse. Great efforts have been made by meta-analysis to bring these numerous experiments into a framework demonstrating an acceptable degree of reliability. Whether the scientific establishment will ever accept probabilistic proof of psi remains to be seen, and, in view of the establishment's resistance to the implications of the paranormal, the prospects are doubtful. Powerful belief systems are at stake, and scientific fundamentalism dies hard.

Clearly the aim of parapsychologists is, indeed, to have their experiments accepted as items in a chain of probative results. But, pending that acceptance, and for what comfort it may bring, it should be pointed out that experiments yielding significant results also take an honourable place as Class 3 occasional events, where a recognised type of activity takes place at irregular intervals. Alongside earthquakes and statistically significant experiments would be a myriad historically verifiable events of the sort that happen from time to time – births, deaths, marriages, divorces, murders, trials, lectures, concerts, levitating tables, poltergeists and highly significant experimental results – the whole pageant of life, things we prove, if we need to, by looking at the evidence.

It is not only the parapsychologists with their statistically based methodologies who suffer disappointment in having their experiments dismissed or ignored as proof by demonstration and end up in what they feel to be the inferior class that has to be assessed by verification. When William Crookes found that Daniel Home could make the end of a wooden board dip down and pull on a spring balance while placing his finger tips on the other end that rested on the table, Crookes thought he would be able to deliver scientific proof of psychic force. He invited the Secretaries of the Royal Society to witness the demonstration. One refused, and the other seized on a small detail in the set-up that certainly could not have accounted for the magnitude of the effect, and refused to take any further interest. Crookes went on to try various methods in which Home altered the weight of the board without touching it at all. As a class 1 demonstration it was possibly one of the clearest ever devised, and Home was fairly reliable in his ability to perform, but, as class 3 reporting, it leaves something to be desired in that Crookes asks the reader to credit him with some common sense. He expected his competence and his word as a scientist to be accepted; but no psychical researcher can afford to make these assumptions, even if he is a Fellow of the Royal Society (Medhurst et al. 1970).

For class 3 reporting, nothing must be assumed, and every precaution taken must be noted, not by asserting that all necessary steps were taken, but by painfully and tediously enumerating those steps, so that they can be scrutinised and assessed by the historical methodologies of verification. If Crookes had succeeded in getting the Royal Society representatives to observe and then to replicate his experiments he would have had, for the time being, a class 1 scientific demonstration. But, with the passing of Home, the whole package (including any Royal Society witnesses and their testimony, would pass along with him into class 3 – things that are said to have happened.

We come now to the singular: the paranormal events that equate with the invading jellyfish; unusual events belonging to no established class of recurrent incidents; things that just happen now and then, here and there. These are in the same class as the less routine facts of history, taking history to be the unfolding of events from moment to moment. Here, above all, it is ludicrous to think in terms of scientific proof. As in all other departments of verification, technology plays a part in dating documents, authenticating signatures and so on. But, of course, you do not look to science to prove that James VI of Scotland was the same person as James I of England, or that Charles I was beheaded, a highly improbable event generally accepted without question as real on purely historical evidence. Nor can science establish the more recent abdication of Edward VIII, another unlikely happening verifiable by historical inquiry. If we can be sure about normal events that are improbable and prone to the evils of falsehood, error, exaggeration, embellishment and other distortions, then it ought to be possible to arrive at the certainty or satisfaction or conviction when it comes to paranormal events.

It may be useful, at this stage, to look at some examples to see how one might go about establishing the reality of some of the past events that constitute the case for the paranormal. And it is in the past that our case lies. If we wipe it out as we go, not only do we eliminate the subject matter of psychical research, we actually wipe out everything we know, because all we know is what has happened in the past. So let us take a look at some of the jewels in the psychical research crown. One can draw up some sort of ideal specification for a Class 1 demonstration of the paranormal – I should certainly say quasi-Class 1, because, in the course of time, it will inevitably become a class 3 event.

I suppose I have to call the person demonstrating "the medium," though this covers a multitude of sinners. The medium would be able to perform a replicated task with a high degree of reliability. He should also be able to vary his repertoire to minimise the possibility that he has a limited routine worked out to deceive. He would be able to demonstrate his powers to several experienced and reputable researchers, and also to other responsible citizens brought in to test him. He should, preferably, earn a living by some normal means and take no payment for his demonstrations of the paranormal.

On the few occasions when he failed, he would be no worse than an actor who, very occasionally, forgets his lines or gives a wrong cue; no doubt there would be a reason, though no one would be able to say for sure what it was. One must say that even demonstrations of chemistry are far from being exact copies of one another, but, in the aggregate, they confirm whatever principle they are supposed to be demonstrating. Has there ever been such a paragon? In the field of mental mediumship the supreme psychic was Stefan Ossowiecki (encountered in the article on clairvoyance and telepathy) who meets all these desiderata. As there has, apparently, never been any other[14] to match up to him for variety and reliability, it is of considerable importance to establish that what is reported of him really happened. It would, of course, be even nicer if there were another Ossowiecki

---

[14] At this point in time I did not know about Alexis Didier (Méheust 2005)

alive today, but then he, too, would be dead and gone fifty years from now. We are all historical characters.

So we have to do here, very briefly, what needs doing at enormous length: look at the man himself, at what he did, and at the people who say that he did the amazing things he is said to have done. So, to recap briefly on the outlines of his career, Ossowiecki was a Polish engineer of high social standing, who performed acts of mediumship to oblige researchers, friends and other people he liked. Most of his work was done in Poland, much of it with well-known and respected researchers. Born in 1877, he was already approaching, or into, middle age in the 1920s and 1930s, when he worked in Paris with researchers whose names are, or ought to be, familiar to us. In his younger days he is reputed to have been an astounding physical medium, but then he turned his powers on to mental mediumship.

As a clairvoyant his repertoire was extensive, expanding to meet the imaginative demands of the inquirer. His most typical performance was to take a sealed envelope from the researcher and proceed to give a very good description of the writing or drawing on folded paper inside the envelope. Under the strictest conditions of control, the researcher would not know the contents of the target paper; nor would he know the identity of the donor.

When I say that he would give a good description of the target writing or drawing, I mean he would, in nearly every case, be about 80% to 90% right, so that you did not need to consult statistical tables to know that he had hit the target. Here is an example of a test organised by Charles Richet, professor of physiology and leading member of the Institut Métapsychique International (IMI), where most of this research took place.

Richet sometimes used target papers supplied by other members of the IMI, or from his family or from outsiders, some of them well known; among them was the French writer Anna de Noailles. She supplied three target papers, each sealed by her into identical envelopes. Richet put each one into outer identical envelopes and handed one, chosen at random, to Ossowiecki, who said immediately that the writing was taken from a great French poet, and he correctly named Rostand. Then he said – and though I do not reproduce every word here he did not say anything that was irrelevant – he said: " ... something of Chantecler ... the cockerel ... there is an idea about light during the night." He also said that below the name of Rostand there were two further lines written. In English translation the lines were:

It is at night that it is good to believe in light.
Edmond Rostand
Verse to be found in Chantecler and spoken
by the cock.

So he had light, night, Rostand, Chantecler, the cockerel and two lines below the name of Rostand). He seldom fell below that standard and sometimes surpassed it. It was almost as if he were reading from a faded photocopy and getting it nearly word for word.

He did not have X-ray eyes, or hidden apparatus, because on some occasions he deciphered scrawl more clearly than capital letters, and he could not give a reading for typewritten words. He could also give a reading if the target was screwed up into a ball; he could describe objects enclosed in a box, or a lead pipe; he was able, in a most fascinating experiment, to describe a sentence written in invisible ink, and, most telling of all, he would usually launch into a preliminary description of the person who provided the target, not only their appearance but their life history and the actions they made when preparing the target material. So how could we account for this performance on a non-paranormal basis, this being the question you have to ask before concluding that it had to be paranormal.

Could he have been in league with target donors? But the identity of absent persons donating material was never disclosed to Ossowiecki. Further, he had no way of knowing which of the three letters would be picked at random by Richet. If Ossowiecki operated by obtaining secret information, we should surely hear that one day he gave a full description of a letter or drawing that happened to be in a non-target envelope, but no such incident was ever reported. So, if we eliminate simple, or even complicated, trickery and also eliminate confederacy, that leaves Richet as the only source or error or fraud or delusion. In the simple protocol of this test I can see no room for error, so that leaves fraud or delusion. Now, if Richet had been the only one to report such marvellous results with Ossowiecki it might be reasonable for some people – especially those who have not read his publications – to think that he might be fraudulent or deluded.

This is where the inquisitorial method is so convoluted. You must, first of all, appraise Richet, and, though he was inclined to make the sort of error that comes from relying on memory rather than checking the records (bearing in mind the vast scientific and literary output of this industrious Nobel prize winner it is an understandable failing) he should surely be appraised as a researcher of the greatest integrity.

That is not the end of the matter, for now you must go on to consider and assess the other researchers who tell the same story. One will be kept quite busy. There were sundry Russian and Polish academics; there was Dr Gustave Geley, director of the IMI, and, therefore, highly respected by a distinguished body of scientists; there were sundry respectable citizens, doctors, civil servant, League of Nations Delegate, the President of Poland and, my favourite, of course, Prof. Barrington-Emerson (no relation). There was a test carried out at the Warsaw Congress of 1923 where the target was prepared by our own Dr. Eric Dingwall (who used his conjuring expertise to safeguard the target) and held by the German Professor Schrenck-Notzing. There were many others. Unless all these people were fraudulent or deluded then why should Richet be fraudulent or deluded? That is the network of logic applied by people who try to determine the truth about a past event.

Let me say, again, that a past event includes one that happened very recently and may be part of an ongoing story. There was, or is alleged to have been, not so long ago in the 1990s, a boy called Stephen Wiltshire, who, at age eleven, was mentally limited to the point that he could not solve the sort of problem that a normal child of three or four might find simple; but he had an extraordinary talent for drawing buildings, and could reproduce a mass of architectural detail with strict accuracy from memory after seeing the building for a relatively short time, and all in beautiful style. There have been quite a lot of idiots savants reported from time to time with various talents – extracting cube roots or making other monstrous calculations – but this is probably a unique case of a fairly retarded boy being a master draughtsman.

So we have, here, a singular event, perhaps the only one of its sort that most of us will ever encounter. Nevertheless, I expect that most people, who have seen this case described in books and on television, quite reasonably accept its authenticity; one would seriously doubt the judgment (and the plain common sense) of those who did not. But the published evidence supporting the reality of Ossowiecki's clairvoyance is much more copious and robust in every way. Nevertheless, pundits who have never heard his name will not hesitate to proclaim that there is no such thing as paranormal cognition.

The creators of these past events often used scientific methodology in framing their inquiries, just as scientists investigating atomic and subatomic phenomena have to use the evidential methodology of lawyers to establish a case. Let me quote from a popular science book by Heinz Haber:

And so, more than 100 years ago, scientists were already hot on the trail of the atom. Hardly a single reputable scientist remained who was not convinced that the atom exists; all believed in the atom, though nobody had ever seen one. Yet the belief in its existence was based entirely on what a lawyer would call circumstantial evidence. It was as though the atom was the defendant in a trial. The judge, the jury, and the witnesses were all scientists. The witnesses brought to court a tremendous number of observations from the scene of the crime, and these facts could only be explained if there was such a thing as an atom. The jury weighed the facts. The circumstances were such that it could only conclude: the atom exists.

If the scientific jury weighed the facts of the paranormal in an equally rational way, they would conclude that Ossowiecki had certainly demonstrated paranormal cognition.

They would draw similar conclusions if they gave due weight to documents signed by 100 respectable citizens (mostly scientists) stating their certainty that PK had been demonstrated to them by the medium Willi Schneider in fully controlled and decisive tests carried out by Prof. Schrenck-Notzing. Similar attestations to physical phenomena were obtained at the French IMI. One must ask how many attesting signatures would carry conviction with someone who was not disposed to accept the reality of the paranormal? If 100 signatures carry no weight would 1000 persuade anyone to accept this powerful testimony against his inclinations? The answer is plainly, sadly, 'No.'

Dr. John Beloff, a past President of the SPR, pointed out what a fine thing it would be if we had a permanent paranormal object (PPO) that could prove itself in that it could not be faked by any known process, so that testimony as to its provenance would not have to be involved in the verification process. There may be objects approaching the status of PPO already in the world, no further away than Paris. I refer to the 'hands' of Kluski. Kluski has figured in previous articles in connection with automatic writing and the production of wax moulds.

Like Ossowiecki, Kluski was a successful professional man who demonstrated mediumship to oblige his friends, though it impaired his health. When he came to Paris in the 1920s he was already well known for materialisations, and one of ways he delivered tangible evidence of this was to get the 'spirit' hands to plunge into molten wax, then to dematerialise leaving a very thin but unbroken wax mould. The spirit hand was able to remove itself without breaking the fragile mould simply by dematerialising, whereas a human hand would break the mould, hands being bigger than wrists. Plaster casts were taken from the moulds, and these show lines, wrinkles and other skin surface markings. The purpose at the Polish sittings, where scores of hands were said to have emerged, was to prove a spirit visitation, but, of course, things were different at the IMI in Paris (Barrington 1992).

Here the purpose was to produce moulds under carefully controlled conditions, providing physical evidence of materialisation. Though it was no part of the design, the casts preserved at the IMI are distinguished by a highly surprising feature, viz. they consist largely of adult hands scaled down to various child sizes. This property, so inexplicable in normal (i.e. fraudulent) terms, was attributed during the Polish sittings to undersized phantoms that indicated 'low power' emanating from the medium, and they could be increased to full size by sitters helping the medium by breathing in unison with him. Though savouring of personal mythology, this explanation has an internal consistency (Weaver 2015)

Scaled-down hands with adult shape and markings, which seem, then, to be a by-product of 'low power' are a very happy accident. For, excluding the 'low power' explanation, how can the varying scales of the hands be explained, i.e. explained away? Though not quite up to the PPO standard in that the circumstances under which they originated has to be part of the evidence the casts showing adult shape and lines at various undersizes remains a challenge to the psi-denier. Not that this would ever be conceded. Explanations would abound, all involving incompetence or deception by somebody at some stage, or several people at several stages. And the different sizes of hand? Some far sighted person in the 1920s might foresee that a century or so later someone might make a big point about this inexplicable feature and substitute a complete range of hands (made from the hands of midgets of varying sizes) for the original ones, which were all made from Kluski's own hands, plunged into the wax while his controllers went to sleep. Or someone will say that he has examined the hands at the IMI and they are perfectly normal size. It would be the same if an unassailable PPO could be put on display. There is always expert (sometimes self-assessed) opinion on the other side, so that the denier can breathe a sigh of relief.

Therefore we must return to the position where the truth about the hands of Kluski has to be established by reference to the conditions under which they were produced, which means we have to assess the testimony of Geley, Richet and the Polish researchers. We have to consider how likely it is that Kluski, or a collaborator, chose to make up wax moulds using several differently sized groups of midgets (rather than more easily available adults or children), that Kluski was able to introduce the moulds into the sitting and manipulate them while his hands were held by the IMI researchers, and so on and on. When all circumstances are taken into account, then the reasonable conclusion may be drawn that the wax moulds must have been of paranormal origin. Ultimately we have to rely on verification by inquisition, and, though a person who accepts the testimony as compelling cannot claim to have an incontestable proof on hand, he can echo the views of Sir William Crookes, who said that the occurrence of the paranormal was as well established as any other fact in life.

It is very understandable that many researchers, especially those engaged in parapsychological experimentation, yearn for the apparent certainties of scientific modes of proof. Verification relies on judgment, a fuzzy concept compared with the clarity of the eyewitness experience that validates demonstration and prediction. The endpoint of scientific proof presents itself as knowledge and certainty, whereas the endpoint of verification is varying degrees of satisfaction or conviction. The unease engendered by assessment-based conclusions reminds me of my early car driving experience, and the shock of realising that when one vehicle passes another the driver cannot actually see the edges of the two vehicles, but must make an assessment of their position and judge the distance between them.

But, as we have shown, the seemingly solid rock of certainty based on scientific proof is extremely limited in scope. Apart from common and daily effects that are manifest to all of us, scientific certainty is available only to those investigators who personally observe the outcome of their experiments. That has to be a mere sliver of experience. All other quasi-certainties rely on the testimony of other people, so that scientific knowledge, for the overwhelmingly greater part, also depends on those soft-centred concepts of satisfaction and conviction based on the arts of assessment and judgment.

So, if in our appraisal of the paranormal we cannot offer 'proof' on demand, let us make it clear to those who do the demanding that the methods of verification applied to paranormal effects and events precisely mirror the methods applied to effects and events in the normal world. If we can feel sure that, as reported recently, passengers in a transatlantic flight were informed, due to an inadvertently broadcast recorded message, that an emergency landing was to be made in the sea and they should put on their life-jackets (surely a most unusual and possibly singular error) then we are entitled on the same principles of testimony assessment to be equally sure that, on repeated occasions, Ossowiecki demonstrated clairvoyance to numerous witnesses. We can be sure that these things happened on the same reasonable grounds, namely, that the evidence compels acceptance. These were real events in the real world, with real implications. Anyone who ignores them on the grounds that they are not the subject of scientific proof is, to put it politely, making a serious category error, and equating the domain of science with the whole of reality.

JOTT – MINOR INCIDENTS, MAJOR IMPLICATIONS

~

It was in the distant days of 1991 that I first named the phenomenon of jott, which, strictly defined, is the occurrence of spatial discontinuity, or, as I prefer to think of it, a stitch or two dropped from the fabric of causal reality, generally regarded as the only reality. Jott started as an acronym for Just One of Those Things. It is a collective word like sport or crime, but can also be singular or plural. A typical one of those things is when you reach for your pen, if you still do such a thing, and find that it's not where you left it – on the right side of the desk, if you are right handed. If it is a bad jott day you never find it, but with any luck you find it, but now on the left hand side, or sitting on top of the refrigerator, where you feel sure you did not put it, or perhaps even inside the refrigerator. Or you may find it a few minutes later back where it ought to have been. Or perhaps it seems to be back in the right place, but is not the right pen. (Barrington 1991)

Members of the SPR and others have reported numerous incidents of this sort, and some of them have been put on record[15] in the Paranormal Review and its predecessor the Psi Researcher, and the whole subject has been explored in a recent publication (Barrington 2018). Most reports of jott are jottles, a jottle being a displacement jott, and this is by far the most frequent manifestation of jott. The other class is the odd jott, more difficult to define. It may be described as a jott that is not primarily a jottle; an article behaves in a way that is incompatible with its physical

---

[15] There is also a box file where they are given reference numbers, and this is lodged with a member of the SPR.

structure, but displacement is not significantly involved, or, if involved, it is not the major feature. For example, if two solid wood rings were to be found suddenly joined together (or *vice versa*), that would be an oddjott – very odd indeed. Oddjotts are rare events, whereas the common jottle is, by comparison, an everyday experience. There are six classes of jottle, all designated with fairly self-explanatory names, and here I shall define them briefly (legal style precision frequently results in a definition that, on the plus side, has only one possible meaning, but, on the minus side, that meaning can be quite difficult to discern):

Walkabout: an article disappears from a known location and is found later in another location, sometimes bizarre.

Comeback: an article disappears from a known location and is found later back in, or very near, the place from which it disappeared.

Flyaway: an article disappears and is never seen again.

Turn-up: an article known to you appears in a location where it could not have been at an earlier time, but (unlike the case of walkabout) its earlier location is not certain.

Windfall: This is the turn-up of an article you have no recollection of having seen before.

Trade-in: an article disappears, as in flyaway, and a very similar (but unrecognised) article appears, as in windfall, as if trying to pass itself off as the one that jottled.

Now assuming that these things do actually happen, as evidenced by the representative cases that follow, jottles may seem trifling, but the implications of these breaks in continuity are far reaching. It has been suggested that jott indicates the existence of extra dimensions into which objects drop in or come out, or more usually out and back in; but there are other forms of physical phenomena that are not so much drop-in and drop-out as peculiar deformations of what one takes to be our familiar three-dimensional environment. I have in mind weird phenomena such as large scale materialisation, in which things and forms seem to evolve and dissipate rather than be here one moment and gone the next, or vice-versa. So I favour a more radical model, seeing jott as a pointer to my own concept of reality. This concept is derived from consideration of the evidence, so it will inevitably provoke challenges when proclaimed as a prior standpoint, and especially when it is condensed into a rather cryptic nutshell; but hedged with these reservations, I present it here before summarising the cases, because, if the concept is well founded, it makes the phenomena of jott credible, and not all that improbable. So here it is.

The world around us is a mind infused material structure advanced through time and held in place by psychic force emanating from a telepathically linked network of human minds operating at their unconscious level. In our task of actualising and maintaining the environment we are given directions, at that unconscious level, by a central control mechanism acting quasi-hypnotically on our telepathic receptors instructing us how to carry out this task, the key directive being that we must always observe strict causality. If we allow our telepathic reception to lapse (deliberately by personal messaging or engaging in séances, or inadvertently, because of fatigue, reverie or other form of inattention) the instructions are impeded and we experience deviant realities, such as séance room manifestations and poltergeist effects, but for everyday, short-lived episodes of disconnection we get the minor causality breakdowns of jott.

That nutshell will be amplified in due course, and enlarged in the talk on Psychic force, which considers the relationship between normal and paranormal realities on a wider front. Meanwhile it is useful to lay down these basic principles from the start, because, if you look at the evidence for jott while believing that things around us are and must be just as they seem to be, i.e. physically immutable and immutably causal, on that basis the incidents to be related here would be resisted as impossible. The same can, of course, be said (and was said in the talk on the repeatable experiment) for all psycho-physical phenomena, because psi can be defined as the occurrence of non-causal events, which are indeed impossible in a strictly realist world where every perceivable instant is consistent with the instant immediately preceding it.

I have used the word 'causal' to mean 'apparently causal.' You cannot say that the blue colour in a carpet was caused by the pink colour adjacent to it, even if you know that the pink was woven first; but it fits into a coherent and regular pattern of alternating colours. That is the sort of causality I mean, where there is consistency from one instant to another, and things in a consistent world don't disappear and reappear in different locations. Most people's assumption that missing articles are due to misperception, carelessness, absent mind, etc., is justified, as indeed it is in many cases where jott seems a possibility. It is fully conceded that there need to be very good reasons for natural explanations to be excluded in favour of a jottle.

The experience of the jottler (the person undergoing the jottle) is that missing articles disappear, but – a very important but – disappearance is a consequence of what really happens (according to the model), which is that jottlings (things that jottle) cease to be visible because they cease to be actualised, and their constituents collapse into the alternative potential state, rendering them intangible and invisible. This is what is postulated to happen when articles that are for some reason neglected cease to be actualised by someone who is in a state conducive to jott. Among those states are drowsiness, abstraction and personal telepathic activity, i.e. sending or receiving personal messages instead of receiving and acting upon instructions about reality maintenance, like office workers texting friends instead of attending to their duties. There may be a lot more careless actualising than we suspect, because jottlers notice an absence only when they are motivated to look for the thing that has de-actualised.

This concept of matter occurring in two states, potential and actual, obviously echoes similar concepts in twentieth century physics. It is not for me to assert that the concept of reality, as described here in connection with jott, is consistent with the concepts of particle/wave form depending on 'observation' in quantum physics as, I hasten to add, kindly explained to people like me in paperbacks and TV programmes. I just note the apparent resemblance.

So after that build-up we come (soon) to some examples of jott, which, if reliably related, are hard to explain in normal terms. Though I have started by setting out a framework within which jott is possible, plausible and even probable, the first essential is to produce satisfying evidence that jotts do actually occur. As we know by now, the authenticity of psychical phenomena does not rest on a prescription for how to make them happen, or to predict their occurrence, as in the causal domain. Argument for their reality rests entirely on good quality testimony, but also on quantity, because there is strength in numbers. But, in a limited space, quantity cannot be provided. Nor can a lot of the detail that would answer reasonable queries and doubts. That conceded, here come summaries of jottles that have been reported over many years by informants whom I see no good reason to disbelieve, and which have sometimes come from people who have taken considerable trouble to send them in: accounts written on personal notepaper before the age when a report could be dashed off and sent from the office computer.

There may well be some inaccuracy, false memory or malobservation to factor in, and the occasional hoaxer/joker (performing to a very small and unseen audience), but we could not function in the world unless in its essentials we did not rely on what we are told by people in general, and we would have very large areas of ignorance. This is an area where it is useful to apply the Siberia test: you ask yourself if, in its essentials, you believe what you have been told or disbelieve it, and if you give the wrong answer (God, Google and other know-alls know the right answer) you will have to serve a term in a Siberian mine. That is a good way to sharpen the attention and focus the mind.

A. WALKABOUT, COMEBACK AND TURNUP

A selection of cases

It may seem untidy to lump these three items together, but they are closely interrelated to the point where some cases might have been classed under a heading different from the one chosen. Comeback has only one location to establish, take off and arrival locations being the same; but in some examples there can be a hair's breadth between a walkabout and a comeback when the article returns to almost the same place, e.g. the same drawer but further back in the drawer. Seldom does an article return with such precision as MG's wife's ring, which returned to its familiar small dish after a few months absence. Turn-up is closely related to walkabout, but its original location is less precisely specified. All raise the same question as to where the jottling (the peripatetic article) was 'lurking' during its absence – if anywhere.

The class references (such as WK) identify some 180 case reports in the Jott file held by the SPR, while the number in brackets indicates the approximate date order in which the incidents occurred. If 'some 180' sounds unscientifically imprecise this is because some of the letters recount a clutch of incidents, some recognisable as jott and some difficult to understand, a circumstance that nearly always seems to go with handwriting that I cannot entirely decipher. Hence the lack of a precision that, if pursued, would exact too high a price in unrewarding toil. And the approximation of date order is because some accounts relate to past times when the date is not precisely known or specified. Many of these accounts derive from the mid-1980s, following an article in the magazine The Unexplained asking readers to write in about their jott experiences. In addition to the selected cases, which have been sent in to me or to the SPR, or published as jott, there are some further cases culled from other publications; these have usually been reported as teleportation, apports or mysterious disappearances.

Some cases of walkabout tell of articles that are found fairly close to the place from which they disappeared, as if the jottling had made a furtive little jump while no one was looking, sometimes giving rise to suspicions that the jottler might have been mistaken as to the original position. There are, however, cases in which the distance 'travelled' covers miles and even crosses national boundaries and oceans. It seems fair to assume that clocks, clothes and brushes do not actually take flight from one country to another. The plain fact is that the jottling ceases to be present at the departure location and is later found to be present at the arrival location.

Some of the cases summarised have been reported, usually at greater length, in the SPR publications The Psi Researcher and its successor (from 1997) The Paranormal Review. Some of these cases will be indicated by a PR and issue number in brackets.

Most of the long-haul cases also incorporate jottle features other than walkabout, depending on the viewpoint of the people involved. The first case to be presented is particularly complex, but it is also extremely well documented. Prof. BSM, of Bristol University, reported it and this is a summary of quite a complicated story set out in a long letter dated December 3, 1988.

WK1 (4) The pigeon post?

> One summer afternoon the professors's wife was sleeping in the very secluded garden of a well-detached house in the Somerset countryside and woke to find an unopened letter on her lap addressed to a Miss X at a west London address. Miss X was unknown to the BSMs and they turned out to be unknown to her. The letter was from a London University college librarian requesting the return of a library copy of Chaucer's works. At the time, BSM had no connection with the university. The morning post had already been delivered to the front porch and there was no afternoon post. The letter was returned to

the librarian, and later it disappeared, as did the carbon copy from the librarian's file.

It will be seen that, from Mrs M's perspective, this was a very mysterious windfall and from that of the librarian it was, later, a flyaway, as the letter together with its envelope and carbon copy all vanished from the file. Though this case is classified as a walkabout, one of the most curious features is that Mrs M's windfall, together with the librarian's copy letter, became the librarian's double flyaway. Altogether a very comprehensive jottle, and one backed by contemporary documentation. For the disappearance of other anomalous documents see the equally sensational narrative of Dr Betty Cay summarized under Windfall.

An American visitor to England gave me a very circumstantial account of a walkabout that made a strong impression on her. This summary has extracted the essentials.

WK6 (60) <u>The remote control</u>

> C., driving through an arid landscape and feeling drowsy, reached for the CD player remote control, but found that it was not in place, though it had been in use before on that journey. Her passenger confirmed that she had not touched it. They stopped and searched the car, to no avail. After dropping her passenger at home, C drove on another seventy miles and, on arrival home, her husband searched the car unsuccessfully. For two months she had to operate the CD player manually, but one morning on taking the car out of its locked garage (her husband having his own car in another garage) she found the missing remote control sitting conspicuously in the drinks container between the seats.

C went to the trouble of obtaining the signature of her passenger to her detailed narrative, and felt that their determined search for the article at the time served a purpose in that she was jolted into a fully alert state of mind. I speculated that she had felt some guilt at cutting short a rather tedious narrative from her passenger that was adding to her drowsiness, and administered some self-punishment. Two months' deprivation of the remote control does, however, seem rather excessively penal.

WK8 (8) <u>Saved from the storm</u>

Some jottles show clear indications of working for the advantage of the jottler, though, on the surface, the incident manifests as a nuisance.

> A veterinary surgeon had agreed to tramp across fields to inspect a bull that her friend was minded to buy. On that day, rain was falling and a gale was blowing. When AMSE went to fetch her keys from the table where she had left them they were not there. She had to telephone and cancel the arrangement. The next time she entered the room she saw the keys displayed on the table where she had expected them to be.

Both women were quite relieved at having a good reason to postpone their visit to a muddy field in wind and rain. It is not often that a jottle is so palpably useful. It has to be said that a negative hallucination would also fit this story, if hallucinations are more commonplace than is generally supposed.

In the following case the article remained unperceived for much longer, and it happened to a particularly sceptical SPR member, who would always seize on any explanation rather than countenance a paranormal one.

CB2 (20) <u>The car parkin</u>

> John Stiles was given a parkin (a sort of rock cake) to eat on his drive home. Being a very slow and cautious driver he ventured to place it on the dashboard, but, when he stopped, the parkin was not to be found. Nor could it be found next day in daylight. Many months later he arranged to sell the car, and gave it a thorough cleaning. At this point he noticed a very visible bulge under the carpet in the passenger footwell, and, on taking up the carpet, found a wizened parkin.

How the parkin could have got under the carpet and how it could have escaped notice before that day remain major puzzles. John would surely have felt over the floor at the time, when he was very keen to eat the parkin (even if it needed a little dusting off). This jottle has, in common with the following case, an element of restoration before some change in circumstances.

CB3 (28) <u>The twin pens</u>

WV, a solicitor, had two Pelikano pens, which he kept in the inside pocket of his jacket. While pausing in the annotation of some papers, he put the current one down on the desk, but it was missing when he went to pick it up. A search yielded nothing, so he used his second pen. His secretary could not find the missing pen, nor did the cleaner. Every morning the desk top was completely cleared for the post to be sorted. A time came when he was to move to another room. That evening, while working on papers for use next day, he needed his pen, and saw that it was already on the desk, though he did not remember putting it there. It was the lost pen, and the other one was still in his pocket.

Like the parkin, it came back just in time to make good the loss in that particular setting. In the following case, long distance and time delay were combined.

WK3 (6) <u>The long-haul hairbrush</u>

On packing for return from Kenya the informant could not find a much-prized hairbrush. Nine months later it turned up on his bedroom floor.

Some jottles seem more pointless than others and this seems to be one of them.

In the following case, a pointlessly wandering mug (WK4 in the file) turned out to serve a purpose, in that the incident was related by EC to a visitor who turned out to have a strong interest in hearing about an article that returned to its former location.

WK5 (56) <u>The necklace on the path</u>

The visitor was a chiropodist who had responded to an urgent summons by EC to come to the house. On hearing the story of the homing mug the visitor said she wished that her gold necklace would return to base, explaining that about a week earlier she had taken the necklace off and fastened it around the arm of her sofa, and fell asleep. When she woke up the necklace was no longer there. The previous day EC and his wife had been handed a gold necklace found on their garden path. It was indeed the chiropodist's necklace. Its relocation from the arm of her sofa to their garden path is wholly unexplained.

Unlike so many jottles that seem arbitrary, accidental and meaningless, this one has all the hallmarks of stage management and orchestrated coincidence. And though the following narrative does not relate a case of jott, I should like to throw in a brief summary of an incident where a 'reason' for telling someone about an incident showed up after the event.

> I once told a friend, DK, who had never expressed an interest in the paranormal, about my experience two years earlier in which a painting in my room rotated to a weird angle while a mutual friend was telling me over the telephone about his dubious poltergeist. He was in a disturbed mental state at the time, and I told him that it wasn't really happening ... but it certainly happened to me.

She listened to my tale with glazed eyes and blank face, clearly radiating I-don't-want-to-hear-this. I wondered why I had told her. Within days there turned out to be a very good justification.

> She was told a much more interesting story about a painting of a boating scene that rotated shortly after the narrator learned that his boating friend had had a severe heart attack. He suspected that his friend had died, and telephoned his friend's wife. While he was telephoning his wife straightened the painting, but it rotated again. His friend had indeed just died.

DK knew she had to pass this on to me. If she had not been 'primed' by my story she would have dismissed his story as not-what-I-want-to-hear and forgotten it very quickly. In fact, a few years later, she had forgotten it, though there was nothing wrong with her memory. She still didn't want to know!

It is argued against the reality of jott that people put things in strange places while in a state of abstraction, as indeed they do; but abstraction can hardly be stretched to cover the following case, reported by a prominent member of the Scottish SPR.

WK 12 (47) <u>The orange washing-up bowl</u>

> While her husband took the dog for his evening walk, DP washed the dishes, took the bowl out of the sink, put the dishes away, and made to return the bowl to the sink, but the bowl was not there. When her husband returned they both searched the small kitchen, without result. After a day or two the bowl was replaced with a new (red) bowl. A week later DP wanted the pressure cooker, which was kept in a lower cupboard where there was a table standing in front of it. She moved the table, opened the cupboard, but found the pressure cooker jammed in place. Her husband came to help and, when he prised it out, they found, wedged in at the back, the orange bowl, still a bit damp with stagnant water.

It is difficult to imagine that at some point between washing dishes and putting them away, DP abstractedly moved the table, opened the cupboard door, took out the pressure cooker, thrust the still wet orange bowl in at the back of the shelf so that the bowl was wedged between other items, replaced the pressure cooker in the now limited space so that it, too, was difficult to move, closed the cupboard door and replaced the table in front of it, all before turning round and finding to her surprise that the bowl was not on the drainer where it had been left. That goes beyond abstraction and into undiagnosed and otherwise non-presenting dissociative identity disorder.

A similar case, where someone of supposedly robust mental state would have had to go to elaborate lengths of misplacement, was reported by the seasoned researcher and prolific author, Hereward Carrington (Carrington, 1952).

<u>Keys found inside a box in a trunk</u>

> A nurse, described as a most methodical person, always placed her keys on the dining table as soon as she entered her flat. One day she did this as usual and, soon afterwards, looked for them, as she was going out on another case. They were not there. She had to have new keys cut. Several days later she needed a cork for a medicine bottle; the corks were kept in a tin box in a trunk to which she had recourse only a few times a year. There in the box was her bunch of keys. She declared that she had not opened the trunk since the day when the keys went missing until she looked for the cork.

Could these keys have been spares that she had forgotten she had? In that case her current bunch did not go on a very complex walkabout but was the subject of a common flyaway!

The location in the next case was not enclosed, but again was not the sort of place where someone would put down their reading glasses in a state of abstraction. It is related concisely by MM, a long-term member of the SPR.

TP8 – (53) <u>Glasses found on cupboard top</u>

'We spent a year in Italy, renting an apartment in a large old house in the town where our younger daughter lives. A's [Mrs MM] reading glasses went missing and she bought a pair from a local optician. When we were cleaning the apartment before leaving, A insisted that I should borrow a stepladder to dust on top of an exceptionally tall ancient wardrobe, and there I found her missing glasses.'

We have to wonder if A's demand for cleanliness beyond the call of duty was because she 'knew' that the glasses were there; or did she know subconsciously because she, in an altered state, had put them or even thrown them there? Are people all around us subject to secondary personalities bent on making trouble for us? I am as certain as it is possible to be that this does not apply to one of the SPR's leading researchers, who would certainly have diagnosed himself. He reported the following comeback.

CB9 (62) <u>On top instead of underneath</u>

DR, seated at his computer, alone in the house at the time, reached for the red-covered telephone index book that lived permanently beside the computer. It was not there. He fetched an A4 sized booklet containing (inter alia) council members' contact details, and used that to find a number. After the telephone call was made he became aware that the index book was now back in place <u>on top</u> of the booklet.

If a cosmic controller is trying to convince us that jottles are really human error, malobservation and false memory, he does occasionally make his own crucial mistakes. If the red book had come back underneath the booklet, that would have left DR, and us, scratching our heads and wondering. But it jottled back on top of the booklet, which had just been consulted.

Some jottles are so extraordinary that they do not fit neatly into any familiar class. This can be said of the following case, related by the American artist Raymond Bayless, who took an active interest in psychical research.

WK23 (3) <u>The responsive coin</u>

> Accompanying a friend into an antique shop, RB noticed a coin that interested him, and, on examining it closely, he noticed a conspicuous scratch. He wanted to buy the coin, but the shopkeeper said it was not for sale. When they left the shop and had walked some twenty yards down the pavement, RB felt something hit his arm and then the back of his lower leg; it was the coin, identified by its tell-tale scratch.

This could be classified as a walkabout composed of a flyaway (as experienced by the shopkeeper) and a windfall for RB, a windfall with a difference, in that RB knew the origin of the windfall coin. From the viewpoint of a third party, it is a very singular walkabout, and unique in announcing its arrival by striking the jottler on arm and leg.

Though jott has only recently been treated as a distinct class of phenomenon, jottles have been reported under other heads. In the context of mediumship they have figured as apports, and in poltergeist cases, where they figure frequently, they are embraced within the general concept of poltergeist phenomena. The essence of jott is that it occurs in the course of ordinary life, and such cases have been reported under various descriptions.

WK14 (A) <u>Lady Vane's estate record book</u>

> Lady V was writing daily about matters affecting the family estate, and she kept the record book in her desk drawer. Next day it was missing. After weeks of searches she consulted Lady Mabel Howard, a gifted amateur medium, who told Lady V that the book was in a locked cupboard near the fireplace, and that her husband would find it. After many more searches Lady V asked Sir Henry to repeat the search of a locked cupboard where there were only a few books. He

took out each book, failed to find the missing manuscript book, and replaced the books, which included a scrap album; when he handled it a large envelope fell out, and inside the envelope was Lady V's book.

Myers reported this as a case of clairvoyance, and indeed it is quite a feat from that aspect, including an element of what looks like precognition. But he did not deal with the question of how Lady Vane's manuscript book left the drawer in her desk and migrated to an envelope stored inside a scrap album (one that had not been opened for many years) underneath other books in a locked cupboard and in another room. He probably assumed that someone had put it there – but who, and why? (Myers 1896/7)

Another treasured case is taken from an earlier publication (Poynton 1975), and it is described in twentieth century terms as a telekinetic recovery.

The homing corset

H. Van Loon was, together with his Netherlands based parents, on holiday in the Natal National Park in 1968. His mother had with her two corsets, one black and one white, which she wore on alternate days, the used garment being laundered on the off day. One night the black corset, which had as usual been draped over a chair in the bedroom for use next day, was gone by morning, and remained gone despite a hue and cry.

When they all returned to the narrator's house in Durban a week or two later, his mother immediately found the black corset rolled up and lying on the upper shelf of the bedroom wardrobe. The servants knew nothing about it, and the hotel had not sent it on. Moreover, crucially, the corset had an array of hooks that had to be tied together in a complex pattern known only to its owner; but the hooks would be linked only when it was being worn, otherwise all this elaboration, quite difficult to accomplish when the garment was not being worn, would have to be undone to put it on. As found, The garment had its hooks tied.

So we have an apparent oddjott piled on top of a walkabout – and with features that defy any plausible explanation. And, as often happens in the serious study of psychical research, it has an irresistible element of farce – altogether a difficult act to follow. Let's move on.

B. FLYAWAY, WINDFALL, TRADE-IN AND ODDJOTT

While it is clear enough that walkabout is the basic jottle, the first element of walkabout and comeback is a flyaway; and if flyaway is accepted less frequently as authentic it is not because it is under-reported. Among unselected reports it is the most frequently reported but also the most frequently discarded. Tea spoons, pens, keys, brooches, ear-rings, and other small objects seem to be vanishing all over the globe, together with spectacles, money and clothes. To make a really convincing case for jott, the circumstances have to be of pellucid clarity, and seldom are. One has lingering visions of an earring or an odd sock clinging to curtains or nestling into nooks and crannies, of food absent-mindedly consumed, of money filched for the usual reasons and of garments left elsewhere inadvertently, borrowed, stolen or given away one day, long forgotten (whether by the owner or a third party) to a charity sale.

We must also bear in mind that though a flyaway may mature into a more satisfactory walkabout it might, sadly, dwindle into a case of lost and found – a notjott. One would not rely firmly on flyaway to satisfy oneself that things jottle, but if things jottle it is quite likely that some of them do a permanent or long-term flyaway, sometimes departing in a very strange manner, and flyaway may, in fact, end up under-represented.

The first of the flyaway cases concerns a very small item, one of the sort that normally is consigned to the unselected. But it was closely described by the late very reliable retired engineer Frank Ducker, and its mode of departure is very unusual.

FY1 (9) <u>The postage-stamp</u>

> FD had just one stamp of a particular value, and he was very determined not to lose this sole specimen. As he crossed the room to unite it with its intended envelope, holding it firmly between thumb and index finger, he felt it dematerialise (not slip) and though he had kept his eyes on it as well as his grip, he saw no sign of it falling to the floor. It was never found.

This is not the only case in which jottlers have felt something cease to have substance while they are holding it. This was reported in one of George and Iris Owen's cases.

(I) The dematerialising knife.

As the owner of the knife was cutting a plant stem he felt the knife losing its substance, and it disappeared. He searched for it very thoroughly several times, cutting the plants in that area back to the bare earth, but eventually he gave up. Returning on impulse about a month later he saw his knife lying conspicuously on the earth in the place where it had left his hand (Owen 1986).

Most flyaways disappear more conventionally, some by falling to the floor. One such was described by Raymond Bayless in a letter dated 3rd June 1988, (PR and Bayless 1972).

FY 2 (2) The paintbrush that fell to the floor

RB was giving a painting lesson to a student in a bare studio covered from wall to wall in linoleum. While demonstrating a technique, he dropped the brush (280mm long and 25mm wide – about 11x1.2 inches – at its widest point), and heard it clatter on the floor. He and the student searched for it, examining room edges and trouser turn-ups, but the brush was never seen again.

In reply to my questions, RB said that the floor covering was dark brown but the shiny black paintbrush would stand out clearly in the bright daylight. Did one or even both of them feel that the lesson was going on for too long? Or does something that falls to the ground unobserved (even though heard to strike the floor) sometimes lose its position in the material world? We must all have had the experience of the thing dropped and seemingly wiped out of existence. Perhaps we need to reverse 'Out of sight out of mind' and add 'Out of mind out of sight' to our store of common wisdom.

Documents of various sorts, like teaspoons, disappear with alarming frequency, but one readily imagines them caught up with other papers, misfiled or thrown away inadvertently. But, in the following case, it was not only papers that vanished, but the whole, substantial, folder. This happened to the late Prof. David Fontana, psychologist, multi-disciplinary author and one-time President of the SPR, and it relates to one of the most substantial articles (other than the more suspect clothes) reported to vanish in circumstances that seem well beyond the bounds of reasonable explanation.

FY6 (40) <u>The red leather folder</u>

> DF kept a distinctive red leather folder, embossed with the name of Coutts's bank in gold lettering, containing bank statements from long past years. He needed to find the date of a purchase. He found the statement in question, noted the date, and then laid the folder, open at the relevant statement, on the table in his study and went to work. When he returned the folder was no longer there. His wife and university age children said they had not been in the study. DF made a thorough search of the room, but the folder was never found.

He wondered if somewhere his folder arrived as an apport, and what the recipient would make of it! Remembering the walkabout letter from the librarian that arrived on the lap of the sleeping Mrs BM, (WK1) he might well wonder.

The final flyaway from the collection to be related here is fairly recent and the jottling article is one of the most substantial to make an immediate and apparently permanent disappearance within minutes of being deposited in a known place. This puts it in the top class of flyaway, because, when there is a long time interval between last sighting of an article and the later awareness of its disappearance, there always remains the possibility, even if highly improbable in the circumstances, that someone moved it. In this case, reported in April 2001, ten days after its occurrence, there is no room for that sort of doubt.

FY8 (67) <u>The four-inch cork stopper</u>

> MM took some dried porcini out of a stone jar, put some in a jug and poured in some boiling water; he then turned round to replace the 100mm stopper, but it was no longer on the worktop. Despite searches by him and his wife the stopper has never been found.

Of course one thinks of circular objects rolling into dark corners; but four inches of cork stopper should not have been all that difficult to locate, if it was there.

It would be a pity to leave the subject of flyaway without referring to Hereward Carrington's flagship flyaway, Mrs S's hat (Carrington 1952). Carrington reported this case in great detail, stating that the six people present on the occasion in question were personally known to him and were respectable, upright citizens. No one else came into the room.

The lady's hat

In the course of an informal tea, Mrs S removed her hat and placed it on the floor beside her easy chair. An hour later when she put her hand down to retrieve her hat it was no longer there. The room was searched, but Mrs S's hat was never found there or anywhere else.

In the days when ladies wore hats at tea parties they tended to be substantial articles, so that, once removed, a hat would need to be placed on the floor rather than on the lady's lap, so not the sort of hat that a gentleman could secrete in a pocket. (Females over the age of ten seldom indulge in practical jokes). And a joker would surely have compounded the joke, and restored the purloined property to its bereft owner, by triumphantly producing the missing hat.

We move on to the reverse of flyaway: windfall, the unexplained arrival of a previously unknown article. The first of these is related at great length by the late Maurice Grosse, and it is a challenge to ready comprehension. But the complexities repay close attention, because they do seem beyond explanation.

WF3 (22) The two extra keys

On 3rd January 1985 Maurice Grosse's wife lost her house keys. Maurice changed the lock, and put the keys to the discarded lock away in a box, accounting for all the keys to that lock. He attached the keys for the new lock to his key ring and that of his wife. Next day an additional key (gleaming and new) was found on both rings; these mystery keys were found to fit the old discarded lock, though all the authentic old keys were still there in the box. The mystery new keys to the old lock bore the name of the locksmith who had provided the new lock and keys, but he had not provided the discarded lock and its keys, and the matrix of the mystery keys emanated from another branch, one never visited by Maurice.

This is a prime example of multiple breakdown in continuity. A familiar element, apart from the jottle-proneness of keys, is that of identical or closely similar articles where one might be interchanged or confused with another; they also seem to constitute fertile ground for an outbreak of jott.

Manfred Cassirer, long-term SPR member and somewhat eccentric scholar, received a windfall of mild interest, though it was far from filling any crying need. MC wrote up his report on 21ˢᵗ January 1986.

WF4 (34) The book under the bed

MC found under his bed a very dust-covered book, dustier than was warranted by the ambient dust level. It was a book on the art of drawing, a subject in which he took a considerable interest, though his expertise was in antiquities. He was certain that he had never seen it before.

The book had no great value, and its arrival conveyed no significance. I always suspect that jott has a point or a justification, however oblique and opaque. But perhaps this was just one of those things.

On a somewhat higher level of benefit was the finding of an acceptable item of jewellery in an unaccountable place. It was related in a letter dated 12ᵗʰ September 1983 in response, like some others, to the article in The Unexplained. It relates to an incident dating from thirteen years earlier, which apparently made a lasting impression on MH, the informant.

WF5 (7) Ring found on top of built-in cabinet

MH was dusting conscientiously on top of a six-foot cupboard, recently erected by her husband. She found a ring judged to be of Victorian vintage. No one could be identified either as owner or source of its presence. So she adopted it gratefully and wore it.

Students of jott must give thanks to those conscientious people who dust on the top of tall furniture. They seem sometimes to be rewarded with unexpected findings. I did not like to ask if perhaps her husband had hidden the ring with a view to bestowing it on another lady, but this would surely have occurred to MH if a development on those lines had taken place over the thirteen years.

When it comes to serving a need, the following incident reported by the late John Stiles was more than useful – it was a veritable godsend. He did not regard it as a jottle, because, though he served the SPR as Spontaneous Cases Liaison Officer for many years, he was not one to invoke the paranormal if an event could be regarded as 'a perfectly normal coincidence' to quote one of his favourite phrases. Nevertheless, this is his second appearance in these chronicles, the first time being for his parkin comeback, CB2.

WF7 (25) The spark plug

> Before he had the car that swallowed his parkin, John was the rather stately rider of a moped, a two-wheeler that relied on a single spark plug. He was en route to his garage to have the vehicle serviced, and he still had a few miles to cover when the moped spluttered to a stop, its plug suffused with oil. John took it out and substituted a clean plug, which oiled up after a few minutes, as did his second spare. He wheeled the moped into a side road to consider his next move, and there was something bright lying in the gutter: it was a new, clean spark plug, of the make and size required for his moped. He fitted it, and rode away. It did not oil up, and he got to the garage.

So, did the owner of a similar moped leave a new, clean plug lying in the gutter? If so, was it just by coincidence that John's moped broke down close to the side road, and that he wheeled it to the very spot? He could have continued on his way, wheeling the moped the remaining mile, this being his only option left. As between materialising a spark plug and having some paranormal cognition of a coincidentally deposited plug, John would prefer the latter. He did however consider it to be a curious, but 'perfectly normal coincidence.'

A most unusual windfall case was sent to me by Alan Vaughan, author of *Incredible Coincidence*, a notable book on coincidences, and it had been mailed to him by a colleague, PC, shortly before he sent it on to me in 1999. It has one unique and significant feature, which will become apparent.

WF8 (46) <u>The other black shoe</u>

> PC had a favourite pair of black shoes, one of which was chewed up by her dog, and she threw it away. She was not sure at the date of writing whether or not she threw away the remaining shoe. One day she found herself having to testify in court, and needing to dress formally she was sorry that she had not replaced the shoes. Shortly after having this thought she found 'her' shoe lying on her kitchen floor.

PC found the corresponding shoe in the cupboard, and wore the pair triumphantly to court. The unique feature here is that the windfall shoe was not dog-chewed. It was in the state that the discarded shoe had been in before the dog got to it, slightly worn but not chewed. Assuming that she did not also materialise the partner shoe, why on earth did she keep it? And did it play some part in attracting a windfall partner? Perhaps we should all hold on to surviving left hand gloves, ever hopeful.

That brings us to the last case presented here, which can fairly be called sensational. Dr. Cay wrote a very detailed account of her experience in the SPR Journal (Cay 1991/2) and I start with her own summary.

WF9 <u>Two transient documents</u>

> 'On 18th June 1991, in the unlikely setting of an Edinburgh legal office ... there appeared two eighteenth-century documents within a bundle of twentieth-century title deeds relating to an old house in which I was interested. The following day, when I returned to the office to amplify my notes, the two eighteenth-century documents, of which one was highly pertinent to my enquiry, had vanished. My brief notes on these documents ... were the only evidence of their prior existence. The missing documents were not listed on the typed inventory accompanying the bundle of title deeds and the staff firmly disclaimed any knowledge of them.'

Salient points that emerge from the fuller narrative are that Dr Cay was allocated a room to herself with a cleared table when she was handed the bundle of documents that had been obtained by the solicitors from the bank. The contents were listed, and the solicitor in charge had checked the contents against the list before handing the bundle to Dr Cay. Most curious of all was that the notes made by Dr. Cay from one of the 18th century documents were found to correspond with entries in the official records of the time, and this material played a crucial part in furthering Dr Cay's researches.

She does not describe the documents, but they were presumably large in size and made of the sort of material that is considered suitable for lampshade construction. If she hallucinated them, not only would she have conjured up a lot of useful written material that was unknown to her before, but also she would have had to unfold and refold some very solid articles.

As related in circumstantial detail in the SPR Journal, Dr Cay's account contains references to documents on public record that could be consulted by anyone minded to check on the authenticity of this amazing narrative. By way of character reference, it is worth mentioning that Dr Cay was well known to Dr John Beloff, a past president of the SPR and honorary editor of the Journal at the time.

Trade in is so very outré that moderately open-minded people may find it a jottle too far – an article is lost (whether by flyaway or simple misadventure) and, shortly afterwards, a similar article appears in roughly the same location. In most cases the jottler is worse off by the transaction, and that was certainly the experience of Dr. Alan Mayne.

TN1 (1) <u>Old for new – the two apples</u>

In his bedsitter, while a student at Oxford, AM picked up a pale green apple intending to eat it, but it slipped out of his hand and plopped onto the floor. He searched for it, but that apple (at least in that form) was never found. Some time later he was having dinner with a physicist friend of his mother's in her kitchen when, towards the end of the meal, a small wizened green apple suddenly fell onto his plate.

As in the case of the lost parkin, there is here a suggestion that a missing article had spent the time out ageing. Possibilities open up, but we shall leave them hanging in the air for now, and look at some trade-in cases with no time-shift ramifications.

Lucian Landau, long term SPR member, reported some bizarre jottles, some with a useful outcome. His wife, Eileen, was a medium, and they seemed to have taken causally challenging events as part of their normal life experience. He had originally been an engineer, and in retirement enjoyed tinkering with machinery, large and small, and he was a sharp observer.

TN4 (45) The hunting horn brooch

Eileen had a favourite brooch, and she would often get Lucian to pin it on to whatever dress or coat she was wearing, so he was very familiar with it. The brooch featured two silver horseshoes fixed to a silver bar with a horn fitted between them that could be rotated and seen through from one end to the other. It also had a rotary locking device, which was loose, and one day the brooch was found to be missing when they came home.

After about ten weeks, the brooch reappeared on a disfavoured dress that had been cast out of the wardrobe and was lying draped over a couch in the bedroom. Eileen was delighted, and Lucian never told her that it was NOT the same brooch, though it also featured two horseshoes and a horn placed through them. There was no silver bar, the horn was fixed in one position and could not be seen through, and only the pin and a loop secured the clasp, so it had never had a locking device (Barrington 1998).

Lucian was perfectly certain that the windfall brooch had not been acquired normally and its presence on the dress forgotten. And though it was inferior to the original it served the purpose of making Eileen happy. It may be the most extraordinary jottle ever to be reported by a reliable informant, and one with sharp powers of observation.

In the other trade-in reported by Lucian Landau he actually profited from the experience. The story was reported to me in letters as each event occurred, so the jottle kept maturing in character.

TN5 (16) The kettle spring widget

When a fairly aged kettle stopped working Lucian brought out the spare kettle but decided to fix the expired kettle. In trying to fit a new spring he dislodged a small brass cup, which fell to the floor. Unable to find it he laid the job aside. About two weeks later when he entered his workshop he saw glistening on the floor the brass cup that he needed to complete the job.

Three months later he was tidying his workshop when he found another brass cup of the same design, but worn and tarnished. He then realised that this was the one that had sprung out of the kettle, and the clean one (pristine back and front), was a new arrival, happily of just the size and design required for his aged Russell Hobbs kettle (Barrington 1993).

This is very reminiscent of John Stiles's gleaming and clean windfall plug, though in John's case it met a real need rather than a mere whim. Unlike the Landau kettle saga the next case can be told quite succinctly

TN6 (59) <u>The wrong clock</u>

VSV, returning from a visit to Latvia, packed her familiar alarm clock, but when she got back to London she found herself unpacking a similar, but broken clock that she knew at once was not hers. Some days later her own clock appeared on the floor in the middle of the front hall.

This double incident has been classified under trade-in, as that is its most unusual aspect, but strictly speaking it is a failed trade-in followed by a walkabout – the walk starting in Latvia and ending in London! There may, of course, be other trade-ins that have successfully passed themselves off as mere finding, as was the case with Lucian Landau's little brass cup until he found the original part; and his wife accepted the windfall brooch as the walkabout original, though Lucian was never deceived. But, interestingly, when VSV repudiated the trade-in clock, it apparently gave up the imposture and her own clock, by all accounts last seen in Latvia, came back to her flat, positioning itself in a conspicuous thoroughfare rather than on the bedside table where it belonged, as if to make a point.

Finally we come to the rarely observed phenomenon of Oddjott, which differs from jottles in that relocation is not the main feature; it is hard to define with precision and formality, but, without precision, oddjott amounts to an environmental anomaly and, without formality, it can be described as matter misbehaving.

I have to start with my own experience, as it was the first time it occurred to me that such anomalies could occur in the ordinary course of life outside the séance room. I now suspect that they may occur more frequently than reported cases would suggest, because things that actually happen are usually accepted as the ordinary course of life.

OJ1 (19) The inside-out duvet cover

My duvet cover was washed and then dried in the tumble drier. It was made of flimsy polyamide secured across its width by a zip. The zip was of fragile construction and could not operate in either direction unless the material on both sides was held closely together. The article emerged from the drier inside out and fully zipped up to the hilt with the zip and tag inside, so that the only sign of a zip was a line visible across the width. At one end of the thin line a pin-sized hole was just visible.

Unfortunately, when I had grasped the meaning of the line and the hole, i.e. this was a completely closed system zipped up and secured from inside, I regarded this as a nuisance rather than as an anomaly, and painstakingly eased the zip backwards by inserting the point of a pair of nail scissors and pushing the zip back millimetre by millimetre. Fortunately I had to engage a helper (and therefore a witness) to hold the material in place. When I had completed the task I realised that I had destroyed physical evidence of an oddjott.

Too late I saw that there were only two possibilities, neither actually possible. One is that the article went into the wash fully zipped up, and turned itself inside out, which is categorically impossible; moreover, it would be improbable to the point of unthinkable that I would have taken the trouble (and it was a lot of trouble) to zip something up that would only have to be unzipped for the duvet to be reinserted.

It almost certainly went in to the wash totally unzipped and, in the course of washing and drying, zipped itself up to the hilt. That it should have ended inside out is of no consequence if it started unzipped, but any argument involving zip closure due to water or air pressure is rendered even more inconceivable than if the zip had been on the outside; for while it is a common experience to find that substantial, metal zips on substantial fabrics tend to unzip in washers and driers, I assert that it has never been known for a zip to zip itself up – and when it is small, fiddley and needs material held together on both sides, it just could not happen. All this dawned on me too late to save the precious article, and soon afterwards the excitement was too much for the zip, which broke down, immoveable in either direction.

Let us pass, without further lament, to the other oddjott to be related here, which did not produce a significant end product, but consisted of an anomalous operation, the passage of matter through matter. The incident was related to me by PHP, retired professor of chemistry, then residing with his wife in a luxurious complex of retirement apartments.

OJ3 (63) The alarm call necklace.

> The professor complied with the request of the management to wear round his neck an alarm caller device that had a stout cord passed through side brackets in a closed circuit. Nevertheless the device detached itself from the cord and fell at his feet, though the cord remained intact.

Most jottles necessarily imply the passing of matter through matter, whether it is an article turning up in a cupboard, another room or another house. But the observation is that the article was in one place and is now in another, not the mode of its passage from one state to another. With oddjott the focus is on anomalous processes rather than on location anomalies. Oddjott does not get widely reported, which may mean that it occurs less frequently than jottles, or that it is more likely to pass unnoticed.

It is a sad fact of life that jottles are much inclined to strike the solitary victim, but, just occasionally, there is some support from a spouse or other supporter. We do have on record a splendid witnessed jottle recently reported by a married couple in the Psi Researcher.

The walkabout shoes

> Mr and Mrs KW went for a country walk, and, before leaving the car they changed into wellingtons, placing their shoes beside one another just inside the boot. On returning from the walk and opening the tailgate of the car, they found his shoes in the expected place, but hers were no longer there, as ascertained by both of them. Next day when KW opened up the garage he found

his wife's shoes on the bonnet of the car, where they certainly had not been when he drove home.

At first sight it is difficult to imagine any motivation for this very unusual display of jott power; but then you may wonder if perhaps Mrs W was not over-fond of those shoes and found her wellingtons more comfortable, but her husband was not so keen to discard a pair of what seemed to be perfectly serviceable shoes! That might account for both being present at the loss (though she would be the prime mover) but he being the finder. Who knows?

Speculation aside, it is that rare bird, a jottle experienced by two people, and it is a happy ending to this brief overview of jott; sufficient, I hope, to establish that there is some acceptable evidence that jott is as real as any other psi effect, and that not every jottle-like incident can be attributed to absent mind, hallucination or, in the final resort, to dissociated personality.

What does it all add up to?

In short, it adds up to what was put forward in its nutshell before the evidence was brought on – that these small stitches dropped from our vast causal fabric point to an underlying reality entirely different from the one we find ourselves living in. Apart from the parallel between the lapse of actual state into potential state and similar concepts in physics already noted, science on a less rarefied level tells us a similar story – that the solid ground on which we place our solid feet consists of vibrating spaces, or something of the sort. So nothing is as it seems to be, and we go through life as if hypnotised into experiencing a solidly materialist world. To reiterate the nutshell proposition, it is not 'as if' but we are, in fact, under a quasi-hypnotic command to imagine, construct and experience our environment in accordance with instructions emanating from the control centre of a comprehensive mind encompassing our universe.

It is actually quite common and unoriginal to posit that there is one all-embracing mind in which we figure as cells, or perhaps as fragments of cells. Most people familiar with the evidence for psi have no doubt about the existence of a telepathic network, which seems to operate on the basis of resonance rather than proximity, and this gives a basis for all these concepts. The causal reality must originally have been ordained and maintained by the universal mind itself, but the implementation has apparently been delegated to unconscious human minds, and humans do not always do as they are told.

Apart from the right to speculate, what might justify the proposition that reception of environmental instructions is the primary purpose of our telepathic receptors? The main indications – that physical disruption comes together with overt telepathy – come from a consideration of physical mediumship. In the days when massive disturbances occurred in séances with mediums like D.D. Home and Indridi Indridison, those upheavals were invariably accompanied by spiritualist 'messages' though, in the midst of physical uproar, they were not the centre of interest. Nevertheless these largely disregarded communications were telepathic in character even though they apparently did not have any personal appeal to those reporting on the physical effects. So telepathic activity might be regarded as preparing the ground for environmental breakdown.

The telepathic element is not mere background support but is primary when the phenomena of materialising mediums, such as Kluski and Helen Duncan, are taken into account. Materialised phantom forms that (according to the sitters) looked and spoke like recognised dead people seemed to have at their disposal some, at least, of the mental content appropriate to the person they claimed to be or represent; this necessarily required a very high degree of mental mediumship as well as physical, whether the medium derived knowledge of the appearance, voice, mannerisms and knowledge of the personages from the deceased, the sitter or the past.

So when telepathy is used on a substantial scale in the acquisition of personal mind content, that is when the physical environment loses its causal fixity and becomes plastic, letting itself be moulded by the mindpower of participants in a highly deviant reality. Any misuse of telepathy (from the viewpoint of central control) diverts the attention of the unconscious mind from maintaining the causal environment, and, while deliberate mediumship may result in wholesale breakdown, a passing state of wandering attention in which irrelevant ideas drift into the consciousness (quite possibly drifting in from other people's idle thoughts), that state of detachment from actuality may result in a mild attack of jott.

Psi manifests in many distinguishable modes, and all militate against a rigid causality. What does jott add to the paranormal repertoire? The most obvious thing it adds is its ordinariness, its unobtrusive slip into normal life, unsought, unexpected, and very easily overlooked. A poltergeist outbreak is a major drama in people's lives; if thunderous knocking comes from an empty room, this is not taken to be just a rather unusual part of normal life. Anyone who has witnessed a materialisation or table levitation would probably have been attending a séance that is intended to exchange normal life for something out of this world. But jott can casually interpose itself into daily life while people are on a country walk or dozing in the back garden or settling down to read. It just drops in without drama as if it is just one of those things that happen and pass as water under the bridge. There is probably a lot more jott around than people notice or realise.

But it adds a lot more than that. If a milk bottle is thrown across the room it remains a milk bottle, a levitated table is still a table, and, if a medium sprouts a third arm or materialises lights that form pairs of probing eyes around which complete heads form which float around the room kissing the sitters (whether they like it or not), as reported by Osty (Barrington 2006) the entities do not become part of the normal world, and the ectoplasm (or whatever) goes back to where it came from. But jott makes something unreal happen to articles in the real world. That is a far greater challenge: a stimulus that leads to and (I hope) justifies the model that was proposed in its nutshell before the selected jottles were summarised. It shows that minds do not just manipulate the behaviour of material articles; mind is responsible for putting the constituents of the material articles there in the first place, and it is up to us to keep them in place and not allow them to lapse and, in our perceptions, vanish into thin air.

This looks like a clear case of mind over matter, a concept that raises some familiar issues. But though those issues remain to be discussed, there is a prior point to be made: when people set out to disrupt sequential causation as by experimenting with physical mediumship, or allow it to lapse due to their inattention, this is not a simple case of mind over matter ; it is minds set on deviant causation in the immediate locality opposing the forces of more remote minds in the telepathic network that are obedient to their instructions to uphold the norms and maintain the sequential reality. So this is essentially deviant minds against compliant minds over what directions to give to matter. This does still leave over the question of how those directions are transmitted from supposedly immaterial mind to matter, material by definition; but this is a problem only if they are seen as traditional chalk and cheese. This is a question to be addressed on the wider front of Psychic Force.

As I said at the outset, jott is, of all phenomena, the most seemingly trivial and the most significantly inconsistent with the simplistic realism so widely taken for granted and so seemingly plausible. But, if psychical research teaches us anything, it is that things are not as they seem – and (all things considered) that is my idea of good news.

A SMALL THEORY OF EVERYTHING

～

As to the title – which has probably been noted with polite or
even rude scepticism – there is nothing wrong with the 'a' or
the 'of," and the 'small' puts things into a proper perspective.
The theory is small in the sense of embryonic; there are some I's that
remain un-dotted and some T's yet to be crossed. 'Everything' may be
slightly overstating the case, but we shall be touching, briefly, on the
origin, meaning and future of the universe- quite a wide field. But I
have heard theories disposed of with dismissive words such as 'That's
not a theory.' My dictionary says that a theory quite modestly is 'An
explanation that one thinks is correct but which has not been tested.'
So the title does not claim all that much, and is more dignified than
'Wild speculation on all sorts of things'.

We must start with a brief review of the key facts, most of which
will come as a reminder rather than a revelation. The trawled material
consists entirely of large-scale phenomena, some very large; for while
I feel a sense of security in knowing that the statistical findings of
parapsychology confirm the reality of psi effects, it is from the palpable
manifestations that I derive the ideas put forward today.

If these articles are being read in the order in which they appear
on the page, then readers will be familiar with the first key fact I place
on the table, the lucidity of Stefan Ossowiecki. 'Lucidité' was the term
his French researchers used for clairvoyance, and one I prefer to the
more spiritualistic clairvoyance. With hundreds of examples to choose
from, it is difficult to run out of cases demonstrating his amazing
capacity to reproduce hidden targets, but there is no need to pile up
more wonders of this sort. It is, however, worth reprising his subsidiary
habit of seemingly rootling around in the past – people, actions, and

environments – in the course of homing in on the target, reproducing this being the only thing that counted as a successful outcome to the experiment. The only time that this searching the past was evaluated and valued in itself was when the occasional sitter did not present targets for clairvoyant reading but presented himself and his life story for Ossowiecki to 'read' as a target.

One generally thinks of telepathy as the faculty that enables sensitives to pick up information about other people's lives, but, in the midst of Ossowiecki's outstanding success with clairvoyant tasks, with finding lost objects and with describing people, he showed a quite surprising inability to read people's minds, including the minds of people in his immediate presence who were actually trying to transmit information to him. Outstanding in this regard was the day he went out fishing with Geley, with whom he had become friendly (while accepting that Geley had to treat him as someone who must be prevented from cheating) and Geley gave him two much-concealed fish scales as a target; despite the presence of Geley, the fact that Geley knew and had prepared the target, and the fishing they had been engaged in, Ossowiecki failed to read telepathically from Geley's all too willing mind that the round, thin, translucent mica-like articles he could 'see' were fish scales.

So, if he was not mind reading, how, it was argued, was he getting his information about people and incidents far outside the scope of any hints that he might pick up from the target or from people present? He actually tells us how he does this, and who better to know what he does than the man himself. He tells us that he imagines himself present when the drawing was made or the words written or the article packaged. He is there with them, and sees the people involved in the task. This does not, of course, enlighten us as to why imagining himself in a place gives him a veridical account of what actually happened at the imagined scene, but he tells us what worked for him. What do we get out of this? We get what is in every sense the no. 1 item:

Item 1. The ability of Ossowiecki is to demonstrate lucidity via a mechanism that looks like putting the videotape of life on rewind so that incidents and environments can be viewed as if he were present as an observer.

On the rare occasions that sensitives demonstrate ESP to any standard it usually seems that the percipient is doing all the work, regardless of the sender; and in clairvoyance the percipient is the only one doing anything. But in spontaneous telepathy it is usually the agent who appears to be the initiator. Could it be that the agent simply sends out a mayday signal, leaving it to the percipient, presumably on continuous alert, to collect the information? I doubt if this idea holds up – and the reader may remember that this issue was the subject of fuller treatment in the article on putting the horse (the telepathic emitter) before the cart (the telepathic receiver) and it certainly doesn't hold up when there is more than one percipient. Such cases are few, but not unknown.

Perhaps the most remarkable is a deathbed case reported in the year the SPR was founded. Mrs. Birkbeck, taken mortally ill while travelling in the lake district, said that she would be ready to die if she could just see her children once more; but her three children were a couple of hundred miles away. She then closed her eyes, and appeared to be comatose; but, after ten minutes, she looked up and said that she had been with her children, and was content. Then she died. On arrival back in London her companion learned that at this same time the children, in a state of great excitement, had insisted that their mother had visited them. One can see how unlikely it is that three percipients would hallucinate their mother at a moment of crisis in her life, and hallucinate her not as she was, lying ill in bed, but as she wished to appear to them. The impulse for that must have come from the agent mother.

The report on this case (Barrett 1882) is very short, and gives no more detail about the incident than is given here. But it does contain the further information that the account was given by an elderly woman who said that she had been the youngest child of the three who had this hallucinatory experience, and that this story was handed down in the family as a sacred trust. Though in some ways Victorians are castigated for hypocrisy and other defects of character (by no means peculiar to them) a respectable Victorian – and Birkbeck is a very respectable name – had a strong sense of probity, and the sacred would have included the importance of telling the truth, so I think we are justified in accepting that this is a true account.

Item 2. Under a powerful telepathic stimulus, information transferred from the agent to the percipient can take the form of a hallucination.

Lingering on the subject of telepathy, can we note that on those occasions when mental mediumship is most effective, there is usually one condition present, namely, that the agent purports to be dead. One need think only of Mrs. Piper's George Pelham control/ communicator, who was able to identify out of more than 150 sitters all thirty of those who had known him when alive and, further, was able to hold appropriate conversations with them. One can think of Mrs. Willett, a woman of fair education but with no knowledge of Latin or Greek, receiving and transmitting scholarly puzzles evidently emanating from the deceased classicist Professor Verrall. From this fruitful tree I pluck the not too controversial plum:

Item 3. Some of the most convincing evidence for telepathy rests on material purporting to come from dead communicators.

Whether medium, dissociated personality or just automatist, one of the strangest contributions to psychical research was made by the American Mrs. Pearl Curran, writing with a planchette, her hand and that of various friends placed on the wooden surface while the enclosed pencil wrote – and she chatted with her friends. Her feat was to produce poetry and fiction of a high literary standard, well beyond her conscious powers and also showing unaccountable knowledge of ancient history. The intelligence behind the pencil claimed to be 17th century Patience Worth and the only effort Mrs Curran put into these hundreds of pages is that she placed her hand on the surface of the planchette (Prince 1964).

Item 4. In a dissociated state it seems that you can create a complex fiction without knowing what you are doing.

I turn, now, from the comfortable notions of mental phenomena to the preposterous claims made for physical mediumship. None could be more mind-boggling than the reports by Dr W. J. Crawford on the Goligher circle. These reports were described quite fully in the article on Making things happen, so those details need not be repeated. It will be remembered that the unique feature of Crawford's experiments was the obedience of the phenomena to the requests made by Crawford to the supposed 'Operators.' This obedience was not only to the effects, so that a request for loud thuds would be met by loud thuds and a request for rustling sounds would also be met, but there was obedience to his expectations as a mechanical engineer. So, as the table rose to the specified height, he would know how much weight should be added to the weighing machine on which the medium was seated, assuming that an ectoplasmic structure emanating from her body was acting as a cantilever and lifting the table. The reading on the dial complied with his expectations.

Apart from confirmation of his main expectations – such as a stream of carmine dye coating Kathleen's stockings to indicate the flow of ectoplasm back to her body- there were small, but significant, items of confirmation. One of the most memorable was that a trademark on one of the stockings that was printed on the heel was found to have moved from the heel to the back of the knee, carried on the surge of ectoplasm. But none of this fits in with reports of physical phenomena in the presence of other mediums, and the idea of ectoplasm streaming from the persons of people present at a poltergeist outbreak is inconceivable. When Eusapia Palladino shook her fist and the door on the opposite side of the room knocked in response, did she suddenly send a stream of ectoplasm to knock on the door?

So, in the Goligher attic, though also on some occasions in Crawford's own rooms, we are as far removed from our familiar reality as it is possible to be, because, instead of odd things happening sporadically, we are in a place where odd things happen consistently. It is like the boutique fantasque, where the toys and dolls come to life, a dreamworld that has solidified into a shared private reality, one that can even stand up to the scrutiny of outside observers. It sounds as if we are in the realms of hallucination, but it is hallucination grafted on to the real world, because, when the sitting is over, impressions made in the bowl of clay by the plasma, which was part of the fantasy, are still there in the bowl, which is real.

Item 5 is the private reality of Crawford and the Goligher circle, where a dreamworld interacted with the real environment.

There are other ways in which a fantasy world can be seen to interact with the real world – I speak of hypnosis. The locus classicus for me is the ichthyosis cure effected by Dr. Albert Mason, a physician who used hypnosis to treat patients. Mason took in hand a patient he believed to be covered with thousands of warts, and, using hypnosis, he gradually cleared most of the affected areas. That part of the cure was permanent, and the cleared skin continued to improve. Later, Mason learned that the young man was actually suffering from a congenital disease and that the cure ought not to have succeeded. Thus enlightened, and somewhat dismayed at having apparently done something unscientific, his subsequent attempts to clear the remaining areas by hypnosis were ineffective. Science had waved a disappproving wand and had destroyed his magic (Mason 1952).

Item 6. We must take note of two systems: 1) the science of medicine, where the mechanisms of cause and effect are known and put to work, and 2) the art of the healer, wart-charmer, hypnotist or other practitioner of the magic arts, where causation is replaced by will. We must also note that magic can sometimes trespass on the causal system.

Let us note another crossing of lines. D. D. Home, renowned only for physical mediumship, operated against a background of light trance and retailing of spirit messages. Rudi Schneider had to become 'Olga' before he could get going with his mediumship. In his early days Ossowiecki would astonish friends by persuading large statues to move around the room, though later he concentrated on lucidity. Kluski, mainly known to us for his physical mediumship, had to be asked to desist from his remarkable automatic writing as this depleted reserves that Geley wanted to put into materialised hands. Gladys Osborn Leonard got rather upset once when she inadvertently produced a hairy arm from under the table, and Eileen Garrett had to be asked to desist from physical manifestations. Stainton Moses, while despising physical effects (saying that they came from 'low spirits'), swung freely from one mode to the other. From all this I deduce as follows:

Item7. Mediumship is double-sided, something like electricity and magnetism; the two aspects can be separated into distinguishable strands but they actually travel together.

Onwards to even stranger things. One of the weirdest tales ever reported to me by someone I know personally concerns a false environment.

Some years ago I decided to relate their story at a conference (that was premature, because it has become much more interesting); once committed, I stumbled happily upon a story related by Jung in his autobiography. Though one is an outdoor event and the other indoor, the parallels between the stories are very striking. In both cases the question arises: were these people in a different place from the one where they thought they had been? In both cases they had just spent a lot of time contemplating a tomb, and thinking about its inhabitant (Barrington 2011).

A tomb is particularly useful for ascertaining locality, because people have only one of them, and this is a good reason to think that the people concerned were in the place they claimed to have been. In Jung's case he went straight from the tomb of the Empress Galla Placidia in Ravenna to the baptistery, while my friends went straight from the Evelyn family church at Wootton, where they had been viewing the tomb of John Evelyn, the 17th century diarist, and came out of the main churchyard gate into the surrounding countryside. In both cases they then entered an environment that did not correspond with the actual location, and both had experiences that could have been directly derived from the experiences of the tomb's occupant. Jung seems to have had a very special empathy with Galla Placidia, whose misfortune was to be married off to a barbarian prince and so cut off from Rome and culture. That this all happened many centuries ago does not seem to have blunted Jung's emotional response to her sad fate. He was already distressed for her before he got to Ravenna, and was even more so at her tombside. What happened in the adjoining baptistery was that he, and his woman companion (presumed to be Toni Wolff), both found themselves looking at four splendid mosaics, which they admired, examined and discussed for about 20 minutes. In every case the mosaics showed a biblical scene connected with water. So taken was Jung by these mosaics he tried to obtain photographs, but there was none to be had of the mosaics he described. The reason for this, he learned later, is that though there are indeed mosaics in the baptistery his mosaics were not there, or anywhere else.

But they might once have existed. He tells us that on one of her sea voyages to Italy, Galla Placidia suffered shipwreck, and she founded a basilica as a thanks offering for deliverance from the sea. The original building no longer exists, but what is the betting that the mosaics in that basilica would have had water as a theme. Jung tells us that he, too, had once narrowly escaped drowning. What if Jung's resonance with Galla Placidia had led him to create for himself a private reality in which he saw the mosaics that were especially personal to her? Of course, if his reality had been entirely private, we should feel less entitled to rely on it; but his companion apparently shared his otherwise private reality, and, later, could hardly be persuaded that their mosaics were imaginary (Jung 2005).

The question that exercised me was whether my friends (I will call them the Wooton couple) might have done something similar. They are both prone to flinging themselves into the past lives of other people in a way that by my pallid standards is positively florid. Biography, faded photographs, inscriptions, old letters – such things set them off. On that day they spent a long time around the tomb of John Evelyn, the seventeenth century diarist, in the Evelyn family church in Wootton. Though they were not the sort of couple who would automatically support one another's stories – he (now deceased) would have been more inclined to contradict – their accounts of what happened next tally and have never wavered. Both agree that when they left the church they came out of the main gate, turned right and immediately climbed up a wooded path, coming to a grassy clearing with a drop on the right and woods on the left. They found a seat overlooking the valley below. At this point the full account goes on to describe a further experience that they would certainly regard as the kernel of the whole story, but this item is concerned only with the environmental anomaly.

The anomaly is that on turning right from the main gate of the church the land slopes gradually downwards toward the railway line; they crossed the railway by the nearby bridge, and for the rest of the day fell asleep on that land. There is no rising ground, no drop and no seat. The whole story, rich in detail, has been related elsewhere, but for now the long and short of it is that I found entries in the diaries of John Evelyn that linked up with their experiences, and eventually found a landscape a mile or two from where they were walking that day (we know where their rather short walk ended) on land immediately adjoining Wootton House, the Evelyn family residence.

This landscape there consisted of a grassed area at the summit of a rising path, with a valley on the right hand side and woods on the left at the back of the clearing, these being the main elements of the non-existent landscape experienced by the Wootton couple. One would not expect a landscape today to resemble closely one three hundred years earlier, and my friend said they were quite different, but the essential features – the upward path, the clearing, the drop on the right and the woods (now huge stumps with trunk sections lying around) were the same. The grassed area would have made a very impressive viewing point for Evelyn, who was passionately attached to the Wootton House grounds. The parallel with Jung's experience was there. I feel that the two stories support one another and form a class: a class possibly related to the more famous and much criticised ghosts of Versailles; so I now add to the pot some of the choicest items, though they may also be the toughest to swallow.

Item 8. The past is still there, as much there as our present moment and it can be accessed by people from the here and now.

This is entirely consistent with the conclusion reached in considering the implications of Ossowiecki's delving into the past when it would seem that he was not doing this by telepathic communion with someone who had personal experience of those past events. He was either searching in something like Akashic records, a giant memory in which the past is stored, or in a mind outside the mind of any individual person. It also suggests that minds from past lives may continue to operate at some level, occasionally exerting influence over people who resonate with them. This may be similar to overshadowing, where a living person seems to be partly 'taken over' by a dead person, and feel driven to carry on the work of that person. An interesting example is the case of the silversmith, Thompson, who suddenly became totally obsessed with painting in the style of a recently deceased landscape painter, Gifford, as if trying to complete his unfinished oeuvre (Carrington 1930).

But, apart from the persistence of the past and possibly of the person, the stories of Jung and the Wootton couple lead to a further conclusion.

Item 9. The projection of imagery into the mind of a percipient may manifest as environment modification, so that under a powerful influence people may hallucinate a personal environment as real to them as the public environment they normally share with the population at large.

Let us move swiftly on from the sublime to the ridiculous: I speak of Jott, which received detailed attention in the previous chapter. In short jott comprises the phenomena of spatial discontinuities and material anomalies, a jottle being the general term for a displacement jott, of which most of us have some experience in the form of wandering spectacles and things that are not where we left them.

The normal explanation, and in most cases undoubtedly the correct one,is absent mind and the other usual suspects. But just occasionally you need the small theory explanation, which is that you are a careless reality constructor, because it was your duty to maintain your personal environment. I feel sure of one thing: if you had carefully placed your keys on the table, and fixed their co-ordinates in your mind with absolute certainty, in the way that you commit an item to memory rather than just putting it down, then your keys would not, could not, jottle.

But just plonk them down in their usual place without paying real attention; allow your subconscious to think up some reason why you should not take the car out – now they can vanish. No doubt they remain in existence as an item in the past, a potential bunch of keys that can serve as a model for reassembly in the present. But for the time being at least you have allowed a material object in the material world to de-materialise, which is a serious matter. It will receive further attention anon. The next item is, of course -

Item 10. The penalty for careless reality construction is a lot of jott.

There are worse things than losing your keys, or your pen, or your glasses – all things that tend to be put down in a hasty, inattentive, disrespectful manner. You can lose yourself. This, you will recall, is what happened to Morton Prince's Miss Beauchamp, who suffered a very nasty shock at the age of seventeen. After that she became a rather subdued young woman, and we do not know much about the next ten years of her life, but then she was referred to Morton Prince, a psychiatrist, because she was a prey to what appeared to be psychosomatic illnesses, or what he called neurasthenia. Prince related what followed in a book for general readership first published in 1905 (Prince 1978). This case is central to the small theory, so its outlines will be related at some length.

Prince put his patient into hypnotic states, and, at various levels of trance, alternative personalities made themselves known, two of them becoming ever more dominant in his patient's life. The personality known to Prince as B.IV was, to simplify some 600 pages, what Christine was not – rough, tough, rude, bad-tempered, described by B.III as "a terrible person." B.III, who called herself Sally, was also a terrible person, but in a different way. She was a sort of juvenile delinquent, pert, amusing, ruthless, and pitiless in her persecution of Christine. A time came when these personages were able to take control of Christine's consciousness at any time of the day or night, when Christine was trying to lead her normal life while suffering intermittent periods of consciousness blackout.

Christine was not aware of Sally or B.IV, but they knew all about her, as well as having their own claimed personal histories and memory trains. They had little regard for Christine, and, if she was looking forward to Christmas or birthdays, Sally or B.IV would take over the Beauchamp persona, and Christine ceased to have a life during those times. She had neither experience nor memories, but would come back to consciousness after hours, days, or weeks and discover that she had lost time.

On one thing Sally and B.IV were agreed: the despised Christine must be suppressed. She was too boring to deserve a life at all. They planned to divide the year between them, and also divide the credit on Christine's bank account, so there would be no more Christine.

They could not co-exist, because only one at a time could take control, but they made this arrangement by writing notes to one another. (This is not fiction!). Finally, not, I would say, before time, Prince took the situation in hand, and using hypnosis again coaxed out a fairly stable personality who had a good claim to be the original Miss Beauchamp, because, unlike the other claimants, she remembered the first seventeen years of her life, and remembered the shock that had dissociated her personality. He realised, to his consternation, that his client Christine was, like Sally and B.IV, a secondary personality, thrown up in the mind of the real Miss Beauchamp when she fragmented.

When the true freeholder returned to claim her property, viz. the mind, body and soul of Miss Beauchamp, Sally, who had told Prince that she would never allow him to send her back to her former state of passivity, agreed reluctantly that she would go back to where she came from. Prince equally had no qualms about discontinuing B.IV as a decision-making person; he had, after all, called both of them into active existence from Christine's trance state. But what about Christine? She came to consult him, but he now diagnosed her to be no more entitled to personal existence than the two squatters he was about to evict from the mind of Miss Beauchamp in favour of the true claimant. But Christine, for heaven sake, was his patient; she had inhabited the corporeal property for ten years, and she had believed herself to have an incontestable right to it. And when she put herself into the hands of Dr. Prince she had not consented to discontinuance in favour of a better endowed patient. But, in the end, she, just like B.IV, had to be evicted, leaving her memories to be taken over by the new Miss Beauchamp and surrendering her right to self-determination.

What do we make of this dismaying story? I think I am a real person, and I expect you think you are. We have friends who think we are real people; but Christine also had friends. If they had all had different bodies the trio would have passed for three real people. They could have sat convincingly round a table, B.IV complaining about the service, Christine looking the other way and Sally planning to put a sticky tart on a vacant chair. Christine did not know that that she was a secondary personality, and, if we were fragments of a larger but dissociated mind, we should not know either.

I ask myself, what happened to Sally when she went back to where she came from. According to her account of her life story she had spent years observing Christine, unable to manifest, biding her time like a genie in a bottle hoping to be let out. But with Miss Beauchamp in command, would she be allowed even to return to her role as observer? Would she effectively die? And yet, if Miss Beauchamp broke down again then Sally would presumably come back to life; which means that though she went into a big sleep, it was not THE big sleep. While Miss Beauchamp lived, so did Sally. Out of this shocking tale comes Item 11, which is couched as food for thought:

Item 11. Suppose that the reconstituted Miss Beauchamp was sitting quietly one day when she heard a street musician play Sally's favourite tune; might not Sally stir from her state (whatever that is)? Put ideas or images into Miss Beauchamp's mind? Remember how it was when she was a person? Make a bid to live again?

We come to another question: however strange some of the phenomena and interpretations so far considered, nothing can match for strangeness the concept of the waiting future. Some people find precognition repugnant to common sense, and, indeed, repugnant to everything else. But it seems to me that a good case has been made for precognition, not least by past SPR President Prof. Archie Roy (Roy 1990), from whom I have lifted 'the waiting future.' Does this imply a block universe, the future in blue-print, or, as Roy suggests, a multitude of potential futures, one of which will be actualised, lit up and experienced? Or are there other implications? The spontaneous cases that suggest sighting of the future are supported by recent experiments in 'presentiment' (involving anticipation of the very near future, seconds rather than minutes) and the unexpected results reported by Dr. Daryl Bem. The evidence may be less compelling than it is for some of the real time phenomena, but it is suggestive enough for the idea of a reality structure comprising past and future, actual or potential, to be a reasonable postulate. At the very least we can assert the following item.

Item 12. It appears to be possible for people to have a glimpse of future events.

The final item may not sound as if it belongs in the paranormal class at all. It is the common opinion that there are far too many coincidences. It is, of course, quite unprovable. We all have our stories, and I shall spare you mine. In one case, however, there are some well-established systematic correlations that, by the standards of cause and effect, seem totally absurd. I refer to the correlations of astrology – not the newspaper horoscope, which is based on the only celestial body that appears in the sky in the same position on the same day of every year – but to the work of those reluctant witnesses to truth, the Gauquelins (Eyesenck 1972). To a respectable degree of statistical significance they found Mars dominant in the natal charts of sportsmen, Saturn in the charts of scientists and Jupiter in the charts of actors – findings that accord fairly well with the planetary influences that would have been predicted by astrologers of old. But can anyone believe that the position in the sky of these planets at the date of birth can have caused any of these people to take up certain professions? Remember that it is nothing to do with season or time of day. Bemused, we have to add:

Item 13. There are correlations that seem beyond the long arm of chance, and cannot be explained on any generally accepted hypothesis.

We have arrived at the point when the assembled ingredients are stirred and brought rather rapidly to the boil. The resulting concoction is the small theory itself, and the lynchpin of the argument is as follows. It is presented as if these ideas were matters of proven fact, but it is actually tendered with due apologies for its speculative nature. That it is fairly consistent with the foregoing tenets is its only claim to command acceptance.

Telepathy is a natural state of affairs; we are doing it all the time. Our subconscious is in touch with other minds both great and small, receiving resonant stations more clearly than others, but receiving over a very wide network. The signals received from this conglomerate (of which we are all constituents) are not normally concerned with personal issues. They are instructions to us from the control centre of our universe (Environment Control) for creating, perceiving and experiencing the world around us; we are, in effect, hypnotised into hallucinating, or actualising from potentialities, a consensus environment, and maintenance of the model is the primary business of our telepathic circuits.

We all have to work hard to ensure that the planets keep to their agreed courses, that apples always fall downwards, that mountains do not move and that suitable discoveries will be made when people dig in the ground, probe the skies or turn their ingenuity to the hunting of the quark. All things must happen in accordance with accepted beliefs and codes of practice, especially when we are looking at them. While Environment Control, like Berkeley's God, is always around in the quad, a tree on a deserted heath might be rather casually sketched in.[16]

This ordering of the material world proceeds from the top downwards rather than from the bottom upwards. The closest analogy here is with the behaviour of sub-atomic forces as conceptualised by experts for the benefit of the non-expert. What comes over, when quantum theorists explain themselves to the layman, is that the electrons inhabiting the atoms that determine whether or not a space is apparently occupied by a lump of coal do not take up any definite position within the possible range of positions until an observation is made. Once there is good reason for the lump of coal to be there, the disseminated essences of potential matter behave like particles and take up positions and motions appropriate to form a lump of coal.

I expect this is a travesty of quantum mechanics, but however misconceived it may be to represent modern physics, this concept of

---

[16] These ideas reflect those of Bishop George Berkeley (1685-1753), in whose idealist philosophy the 'material' world was a thought in the mind of God. This gave rise to a limerick positing that an unobserved tree would 'cease to be when there's no one around in the quad.'

forces ordering themselves so as to conform with observers' requisitions is exactly what I envisage to occur in response to the chain of command initiated by the hypothesised Environment Control, which tells us how to manipulate matter. If we act as instructed, the material constituents of reality will do our bidding and give us the world we recognise.

As well as receiving information we are also continually transmitting our own data to the information pool, describing what we see and hear around us, occasionally sending in an anomaly, for which we would receive a disciplinary rebuke from Environment Control. We then have to make a reappraisal of what we thought we saw, being under strict instructions to maintain consistency at all costs. (If we cannot make things conform then at least we are told to forget about the anomalous incident as soon as possible).

This instantaneous back and forth combines in a personal directive on how to construct our own immediate environment. This, too, may have a few dusty corners where there is some degree of inattention to detail, but the perceived environment must conform with the hypnotic commands of Environment Control.

The perception package is not just tendered; it is pressed firmly and (almost) irresistably into place, the clearest items relating to instant use, while the vast and hazy bulk of it is for subconscious absorption. Environment Control is not concerned with knowledge or abstracts but with incident and experience. It does not need to give us lessons in epistemology or calculus, I'm glad to say; we just need to know what has happened, what is happening and what ought to happen in accordance with the agreed rules of existence, and we do not need to know why.

With all this front page news to be processed the telepathic circuits have a full time job to do, and the task is becoming ever more onerous, with galaxies to be kept going at one end of the scale and elusive vibrations at the other end. I see this class of information as equivalent to the international news and informed political comment – the sort of thing most people pass by with averted eyes. But even the local and parochial news, which most people find much more exciting, is dauntingly complex these days.

For obvious reasons there is a strict rule that news items of a personal nature are not allowed to intrude on these busy circuits, though we do sometimes try it on. But, just as parking a car gets ever more difficult with increased traffic, so also does unauthorised use of the telepathic network. In times past the telepathic centres did not have to work so hard. There was more slack, so that breaking in to the system (episodes of crisis telepathy, such as the Birkbeck case) was more easily accomplished.

Pressing on, I further hypothesise that misuse of the lines takes two forms. In one case the misuser suspends reception of environmental instructions, whereupon his immediate reality becomes plastic, and we may get a Goligher circle. In rarer cases we get false environments and interference with causal effects in the consensus environment, as in the hypnotic cure of ichthyosis.

In the other case the misuser suspends transmission of his own immediate data, which (according to the theory) frees part of the telepathic mechanism allowing it access to the normally forbidden personal material. But, as physical and mental mediumship belong on the same coin, the suspension of transmission facilitates similar defaults in reception so promoting some degree of breakdown in physical reality.

In either case the anomalous outgoing signals, or the anomalous lack of them, alert Environment Control to what this very busy body perceives as a pathological condition and precursor of insanity. It raises its defences, marshalling its disciplinary forces, and, in the course of time, mediums, instead of rising to ever greater heights, start to lose their powers, effects go into decline, methodologies fail, the will to replicate past achievements is undermined – and eventually normal business is resumed.

Apart from those mediums and researchers who, for the time being, defeat the system (and ever greater ingenuity is required) there are those ordinary members of the public who occasionally stumble upon the art of getting free telephone calls; if they receive personal messages with reasonable finesse, no one notices those small slips in continuity that may result from inattention to reality construction duties. Others are less skilful. Even those of us who have no paranormal gifts may find ourselves in possession of stray images that seem to have arrived from nowhere, like meaningless talk on a crossed line. We come out of a sightly distrait state of mind to find that the pen is no longer there, and we are charged with careless hallucinating. Deprived of its structural underpinning, the pen, like a deflated balloon, has ceased to be identifiable, and so probably have a few more unconsidered trifles from which the breath of life has seeped out.

Seen in this light, the paranormal is on a continuum with the normal. The normal world around us is the grand hallucination in which we all participate under compulsive guidance, but here and there, as tiny pimples on its surface, are the local hallucinations that come and go in defiance of the rule of law. As we have seen, people under the influence of powerful personal intrusions into the mind may become subject to large scale and persisting alternative hallucinatory realities, as appears to have happened to Jung. He was responding to the quasi-hypnotic influence of a sixpence-sized mind, that of an individual who, for a limited time, affected him very closely, instead of to the more distant moon-sized Environment Control.

Alternative realities somewhat resemble ambiguous drawings – not the simple cube or staircase that flips, but the much more evocative 'Wife and Mother-in-law,' where the flip is between the old woman with a shawl who is suddenly replaced by a young girl with flowing hair that was once a shawl. You cannot see both at once, but they both exist.

The point is that both realities are potential, both utilising the same material, one image asserting itself at one time and the other suddenly supplanting it. Is there room in our world for potential alternative images? Bearing in mind the prodigality of matter, I see infinite scope for manoeuvre. A few billion particles transferred from a permanent human to a transient phantom would not make him look or feel any different, though he might remark on a cooling breeze (a sensation frequently noted by sitters when physical manifestations are reported).

In the relationship between normal and paranormal, it may be useful to imagine a dazzling light streaming through a slit between curtains of enormous height. Our mind's eye is glued to this slit, because this is the chink through which the consensus reality data streams in. It can also be seen as the area below a very narrow curve with a very high peak; on each side of the curve a little light comes through at the lower edges, but, as you move from the central point, the light that comes through further along diminishes, though it never reaches absolute zero. And what is all that about? The chink in the middle – the narrow slit represents the present moment – which makes it a very thin white line; very thin indeed. Nothing can, in fact, be thinner than the present moment, for this state in which we permanently find ourselves is a mere interface dividing the past from the future. This is now – that was. Here comes another now: gone.

When our telepathic circuits process information about how the world is supposed to look here and now this is essentially a message about bridging between the past and the future. This gives rise to the question: 'Where does the bridge stop on each side of the imaginary line that we call the present?' The answer must be that it doesn't stop anywhere. Under the curve that gives us data for our experience of the present there creeps, however faint and remote from accessibility, all the data of the past and the projected data of the future, the votive basilica of Galla Placidia, the thin musical lady, all our yesterdays, some of our tomorrows.

So when Ossowiecki went on a ramble in the past, looking over Geley's shoulder to try to see what he was writing in invisible ink, he had suspended his data transmission duties, and so was able to swivel part of his telepathic eye away from the central slit with its dazzling signals pressing the here-and-now on us, and run his eye along the bottom edge of the curve, using his psychometric object, the target paper, and perhaps also Geley himself, as an Ariadne's thread rooted in its past to draw him to it.

This may be the method by which ESP generally operates when there is no urgent telepathic message initiated by an agent in need. In a crisis case, signals of such potency are sent in to Environment Control that its present-time data carrier wave becomes modulated in the direction of the intended percipient, with the subliminal personal information hitching a ride, so to speak, on the environmental data coming through the central slit. In most cases these faint signals will go unperceived; but, on very rare occasions, they will lock on so precisely that the percipient may experience telepathy in the extreme form of a modified environment, as seems to have happened to the Birkbeck children.

When one considers the *modus operandi* of a mental medium on the Piper or Willett model we see a process that may be an amalgam of an active venture into the past and a passive receipt of information emanating from an agent. People do not usually think in terms of a trance medium hallucinating a modified environment when she brings communications, but trance states, heavy or imperceptible, mediumistic, hypnotic or auto-hypnotic, are close siblings, so that a medium perceiving words and imagery, or experiencing identity fusion, can reasonably be regarded as being in a hallucinatory state. In such cases I see data creeping in under the side fringes of the curtain, bringing with it material flung out from the mind of a communicator who has been excited into activity in the same way as an agent in crisis telepathy. That material is worked on by the organising powers of the medium's subconscious and emerges duly processed.

We now return to Ossowiecki where we left him looking over Geley's shoulder, for there is another lesson to be learned here. The point is that he did not look through Geley's eyes, or he would have found the eyes focusing on the passage to be copied. Still less did his mind get inside the mind of Geley on this occasion any more than when he was puzzling about the things that looked like fish scales.

Just as he told us when asked, he worked by rolling back time; but he did this as a spectator. Strolling around in the past (and perhaps also occasionally in the future), even as a non-participating viewer, raises queries even more fundamental than does playing around with the fabric of the present. People who react adversely to the block universe usually feel happier about what might be called the growing block, in which every layer of the past persists, overlaying the one that preceded it, so that the past, at least, is there just as the present is there, though normally inaccessible. The idea of the recorded past has a long history, with familiar examples being the recording angel's book of the Dies Irae and the Akashic records of Theosophy.

Ontologically speaking I can make no sense of time machines, celestial video rewind, turning the pages of the Great Book, plugging in to a switchboard, pulling out a disk from the Akashic Records or whatever. The only way in which people outside science fiction can travel back into the past is within a memory system. For that we need, as I see it, a higher order of memory and an entity whose memory it is: an observer who sees all and remembers all. An entirely passive spectator is not the model I have in mind. There is another sort of observer who not only takes cognisance of what is happening but is also, to some extent, responsible for its enactment.

First cousin to the disturbed multiple personality is the happy automatist, who puts out a hand and receives a script, apparently written by someone else inside her head. If she is that happiest of all automatists, Mrs Pearl Curran, she may receive writing by her hand that is somewhat over her head. She may not know what the script is until she reads it, but at least she is the copyright holder. She is an observer, but she is also an author.

When authors plan they look ahead; if the whole point of the story is a premature death then that character will surely die young. Perhaps a baby was going to die a cot death, but the author finds herself allowing it to survive – but only to be run over as a toddler. Here is the basis for precognition and for precognition avoidance. A warning that leads to vigilance and rescue reflects a storyline that changed because the characters seemed to take over and write the story differently. Glimpses of the future look like forward planning by an author, and especially by one who is not in total control. And, just as the future draft can be modified, so, possibly, can the past be elaborated. What has happened cannot be undone, but there is room for speculation-driven detail to be added.

The time has come to ask what sort of author might be held responsible for the drama in which we find ourselves? Two undeniable virtues are his artistry and ingenuity. We have breathtaking landscapes and also those breathtaking coincidences that have been noted. One can see no possibility of a causal connection between having Saturn up in the sky and a scientific career down here on earth; but then there is no correlation between a baby and a stork until someone makes up a story connecting them, and there is no necessary correlation between B flat and the triad on C until someone has the insight to use a seventh to enter another key.

If an artist of extraordinary ingenuity is crafting the music of our spheres he will surely want to astonish us with his correlations. And we do take great delight in tricks of this sort. One of the charms of lyric poetry used to be that it rhymed. A rhyme adds nothing to the sense (though it may in some measure dictate the sense) but it adds an aesthetic value of its own. The correlations of astrology may be the cosmic equivalent of a superbly executed strophe. The fiction in which we find ourselves may be an unedifying sort of video nasty, but who can deny that it is put together with all the skill and cunning of a master craftsman, masterly even when he is dreaming, dissociated, or in a trance.

In a world of lyric poetry and sweet music, telepathy between creatures in the same dream would be both natural and pleasing; we should have direct experience of other people's melodious phrases even when we are just counting rests. But in our world it is just as well that the telepathic circuits are kept busy maintaining reality, because we should all go insane if we had to spend our conscious time blocking off the shrieks of pain and distress that we should otherwise hear from those who have fallen foul of our creator's flair for drama, or his awful sense of fun.

Before we take this theme further we must ask who is responsible for the material that flows from the pen of an automatist, or even from the pen of conscious authors who believe themselves to be in charge. Where do coherent narratives come from? It appears to be a two-way process, in which the one in charge provides the raw material, whereupon the subordinates down in the unconscious take over, getting down to work like those fairy tale creatures who come in at night and do the sewing and other chores while the householder sleeps. Finally they make up a rough draft ready to be unfolded in the mind of the master.

Who are the night-weavers in the mind of our immediate creator? I take it that we are. It is true that we also have smaller weavers in the mind (such as the clerk who searches the memory for lost words and names while we think about something else), but, as I see it, we are the first level of creation that can imagine things being other than what they are. We are also, arguably, the first level of creation that has a concept of immortality, and, if there is any immortality going, we want to be part of it – anyway, some of us do – and, if the past is not wiped out, then we have our small portion. But is there any way in which we can be brought into the memory of the system where we are filed, and hear our own voices again, sing a few notes to reassure ourselves that we are still there?

At this point let us remember Sally Beauchamp, who might have been recalled from her big sleep by something in the new Miss Beauchamp's life that had a particular resonance for her. If the past continues to exist in the all-enveloping memory, it may be that we can think people from the past back into further experience of life; or, that a close rapport, whether or not through a medium, could enable the memories and dreamstates of the dead to become available to the living.

Are we presuming too much for ourselves? In the course of his protracted treatment, Morton Prince called up a lot of subsidiary hypnotic personalities who were deemed by him to be mere fictions, exercises in role-playing, and they were returned to the vat, so to speak, for melting down. Could this mean level of pretension be our true status in the scheme of things? But, even so meagre a claimant existed as an attribute of the total personality, so if Miss Beauchamp can make a bid for immortality they go along with her, small though their claim might appear to be. Our claim in the face of the cosmos seems very small indeed, but what matters is the size of our master's claim.

Time does not allow much to be said about the maker of earth, the designer in whose mind we are destined to merge, and who will one day, fortunately, be absorbed into a higher personality. The Manicheans were quite clear that this world was the creation of a malevolent personage, and I'm sure they were right. We are all familiar with Sod's law; the maker of earth is surely Sod himself, a consummate artist, as we have seen, deviser of beautiful things like spider's webs, and also the deviser of creatures that wrap up their prey in sticky threads and eat their victims alive. What sort of a world creator would make biological arrangements like that? Presumably the sort who thinks it amusing that a turtle once turned on its back can never right itself. Let us hope – and some people might even pray – that the maker of earth has not been allowed to play any part in the making of heaven.

Well, of course he hasn't. He is a mere Sally to a much nicer Miss Beauchamp, who in turn is a constituent of a larger, all-embracing benevolent, or at least sympathetic entity: the one and only ultimate mind, a mind always dissociated in some degree, erupting periodically from near integration and timeless unity into terrifying multiplicity. No doubt there are other dramas going on in the universe, and I expect that they are all tragic and comic, or tragi-comic in their different ways, for dissociation always means trouble and strife.

Assuming the Cosmic Mind to be a helpless dream state spectator of these awful struggles then she (and so fruitful a being must surely be 'she') she will be in what one might call two minds: in her not very lucid dream state she will be enjoying the spectacle of life on earth, and perhaps elsewhere, in the same way that we 'enjoy' shedding tears over King Lear and the St. Matthew Passion, but, at the same time, she will have to bear the inconceivable burden of knowing that all the suffering of these creatures who come to consciousness has been caused by her act of multiple dissociation.

Why would she do these acts of dissociation, giving rein to hierarchy of lower 'personalities' and their creations? One must ask what would be the alternative to dissociation: to go through eternity in a state of endless perfection? It sounds attractive in some ways – everything at peace and rest and seamless undifferentiated bliss. But in a perfect state of integration the cosmic mind would be the only entity in the universe. And who would want to be that ? Perhaps the answer is that the all-embracing Cosmic Mind never has been integrated for more time than it takes to pass over the present moment, so has only momentary experience of that awful solitary state, and then passes again, instantaneously, into a state of dissociation.

~

So ends the small theory of everything, in a ramble up in the clouds of speculation. It does, indeed, cover everything, in its way, because one thing has led to another. The same data could, no doubt, lead in other directions, less way out, more grounded and better supported than the one placed on offer here. It is only a small theory.

PSYCHIC FORCE

~

'**P**sychic force' was coined by Sir William Crookes in 1876 to describe experiments with the medium Daniel Dunglas Home in which Home, among many other (more dramatic) things, made the free end of a wooden plank tilt down (Medhurst et al. 1970). The plank was laid on a tabletop with one end extended beyond the edge of the table, and Home placed his hand on the end that rested on the table, and willed the other end to dip. Later he simply held his hand above the plank. Psychic force is still a fairly self-explanatory term for the concept of mind over matter. The more familiar PK, like its sibling ESP, was originally associated with statistically evaluated experiments; people were required to direct a hypothetical jet of psychokinetic power at objects like little steel balls to urge them into slightly abnormal trajectories. The term PK was preceded in older literature by telekinesis – propulsion at a distance – and neither is apt to cover materialisation, a very different expression of psychic force. We can leave the less familiar Greek derived psychoboulia, for which I have a lingering affection, to rest in peace.

I am not focusing here on the presentation of a lot more cases to prove the point that psychic force is a real effect, but I am asking the dreaded question of how, not if but how, might it operate – so prepare for a rather heady concoction of speculative ideas, which are not susceptible of proof, but which are compatible with the various types of physical phenomena that seem to be related to people's wishes, spoken or unspoken, sometimes related to conscious willing, though seldom under conscious control.

The life blood of psychical research is the personal experience, and it is especially exciting when it is put on record soon after its occurrence by someone you can rely on to tell the truth as he or she believes it to be, and to get it substantially right, so that in its essentials it corresponds with historical fact. We are always being told by psychologists that this is not possible, but, allowing for a small margin of imprecision, I think it is, and so does anyone else who wants to know what is happening in the world, including, as I have argued before, in spheres of science outside a researcher's own area of expertise and competence. Believing in the essentials of what people tell you (which is entirely different from belief in a dogma) is the norm, and, while that belief is properly subject to displacement by reference to the reliability of the informant, it should not be discounted because of the strangeness of the content. 'Accept' is a more appropriate word than 'believe,' but, though there could be a word such as accepter or acceptor in common use, there is not, so 'believe' has to cover both belief in dogma and acceptance of testimony, and acceptors of the evidence for psi will find themselves classed as believers. And, unfortunately, convicts are not people who are convinced. This ramble into the deficiencies of language is not entirely irrelevant, because misleading words can transmute into misunderstood concepts and misconceived ideas.

So long live the much-disparaged anecdote, from which one can learn so much from so little. Remember my favourite, the dialogue between Louisa Rhine and the child Betty, playing on the floor, whingeing about not being taken to the cinema and, without being aware of it, picking up her mother's silent thought and making a comment on it that was more like a continuation of her mother's thought than one to be expected from a young child. As I see it, this tells us a lot more than the collected card experiments of her more famous husband – the osmotic relationship between mother and child, the escape of private thoughts, the impingement of telepathically transmitted material direct to the unconscious, the equally unconscious exteriorisation of ideas relevant to that material – one could write a book about that little incident. And does it have a bearing on psychic force? It has a bearing on all psi manifestations, because it shows so decisively that, whether we are talking about psychic input or output, these processes take place at an unconscious level of the mind.

The following anecdote shows this unconscious power making use of psychic force to advance a consciously desired goal, though the means to the end was not at all consciously desired. The source of this anecdote was what Myers would have called "a person well known to me", and she told me about this incident that happened to her husband before they were married. EB, the psychic force activator in this case, was very wary about anything paranormal, and he did not want it to happen to him, though it did, more than once.

He had recently had a falling out with his girlfriend, who had told him, rather ominously, that she had written him a letter. He feared that this was going to be goodbye. While awaiting his fate he heard the sound of letters being delivered, and, while he was picking up what he saw was the awaited letter, the doorbell rang, and he flung the door open in the improbable hope that it was she, come to retrieve her letter. But no, it was a friend who strode in cheerfully and seated himself beside the fireplace. EB propped the letter carefully on the mantelpiece, resumed his seat on the side opposite the unwelcome friend, and made desperate attempts to join in a conversation. All he wanted was for the man to get up and go so that he could read the letter.

When you play a part in making things happen, those things don't always work out exactly in accordance with your wishes. What happened was that while the friend continued to sit there and talk, the letter, which had been placed in a central position leaning against a clock, floated gracefully sideways and, to EB's dismay, landed quietly on his lap. This incident seems to tell us pretty clearly that PK operates through the unconscious, and, though the operation may have a strong relationship with the concerns of the conscious mind, as in this case, there is by no means a correspondence. EB did not issue a request to the letter to float into his hands, though that was basically what he wanted, but he did not want it to arrive in such a way as to make him (as he saw it) look embarrassingly freaky in front of his talkative friend. If Louisa Rhine's story tells us, alarmingly, to be careful what we think, EB's story tells us to be careful what we wish for in case it is realised in a disconcerting way. But it worked: the bemused friend did very soon find that it was time to make a move.

Another case in which the unconscious took over and did things in its own way was Ian Stevenson's 'telepathic impression' case of the shipwrecked couple who appeared to their estranged daughter-in-law as stretching out their hands in a gesture of supplication. While it is true that in anticipating imminent death the couple greatly regretted the estrangement with their son and his wife, and felt that it would be very sad to perish without a rapprochement, this was not an attitude they would have struck if they had been offered a sort of psychic Skype enabling them to appear on their daughter-in-law's computer. But the unconscious apparently knew how to get a result – she told her husband about her persistent vision, he instigated a rescue and there was a family reconciliation. Reconciliation is an abstract idea, not all that easy to convey telepathically, but a pleading gesture was something that could make a forceful impact, and it did. It seems that sometimes, perhaps often, Unconscious knows best.

In EB's case, the emotional force was directed at longing to get at the letter rather than directed at the chatty friend who was preventing that from happening. In the Stevenson case there was yearning for reconciliation that activated the telepathic vision. Those are not the most usual sort of emotions to trigger episodes of psychic force, because the emotions that stand out as chief promoters of such incidents are anger, hostility and aggression, feelings that in the interests of civilised behaviour are suppressed, but seethe below the surface. One of my poltergeist attractors, a woman who never uttered a swear word or even raised her voice from its calm and measured tones (a form of polite behaviour that can be extremely irritating) was suddenly confronted by her husband with an ostensibly harmless remark that aroused in her a storm of emotions, definitely including anger, hostility and aggression. Were she less well behaved she would have hit her husband, or at least wanted to, but, as that was literally unthinkable, her unconscious took over – she silently blew her top and hit the roof, by which I mean that there was loud and furious knocking on the ceiling a foot or two above their heads, as reluctantly confirmed to me by her bemused husband, a man of science confronted by the unscientific.

They were standing on the top landing, having just completed a job of redecorating, so above that ceiling was the attic. The husband's remark was that the next job was to clear out the contents of the attic, and get rid of the old pram and other baby things, as he put it, so the effect of the knocking was as if there had been a violent protest from the attic itself: a remarkable case of a frustrated woman's anger, hostility and aggression being sublimated into a display of psychic force (Barrington 1969).

That was entirely unconscious causation, but I was actual witness to a case where conscious and unconscious worked together, this interconnectedness being, I think, one of the things that enable physical mediums, occasionally, to have some degree of direction over their powers. This was with Matthew Manning in experiments carried out in the 1980s at City University. In short, some experiments with clairvoyance had not been very successful, and Matthew was furious with himself and anyone else who happened to be around. That was me, left to sooth him while Anita Gregory went away to prepare for the next experiment. Matthew did not like to be kept waiting. I tried to cheer him up by pointing out some interesting connections between the targets and his responses in the clairvoyance experiment, but I think he thought I was taking the mickey, and the tension tightened. I was afraid he would go home, and I would be blamed for annoying him.

But, instead, he mooched over to a device where an infra-red beam had been set up, waiting like the sword in the stone for him to feel in the mood to interrupt some of the infra red and lower its voltage by projecting our old friend ectoplasm into it. So, instead of taking it out on me, he took it out on the infrared beam, and, when I saw the voltage gradually sinking, I called for the others to come and watch. We were treated to a spontaneous demonstration of extraordinary evidential value, the voltage going down by about a third, and generally fluctuating with his proximity to the apparatus and degree of attention given to it. When normality was restored, all were agreed that there should be a repeat performance next day, when everyone would remember not all to talk at once.

You can probably anticipate the outcome – next day, when I was not there, absolutely nothing happened. The others implored me to come back and annoy Matthew again, but my presence didn't annoy him any more, so there was never a repeat performance. But I had served a noble purpose: with my participation in an unsuccessful clairvoyance experiment and further irritant remarks I had provoked anger, hostility and aggression, and these states of mind had sublimated into a demonstration of psychic force, recorded for all time on a chart by the chief technician of Prof. Ellison's department, who became a member of the SPR after that demonstration of psychic force (Gregory 1982).

What it is that supplies the motive power to mediums remains a mystery. With Matthew Manning, suppressed anger spurred him to action, and another spur may be the ignominy of failure. I was told by Dr Hubert Larcher, the chief executive of the IMI for many years, that when he and colleagues asked a veteran medium, Olga Kahl, if she could still respond to clairvoyant target diagrams by showing the response on her skin, they said after half an hour of waiting that they would give up the attempt – whereupon the symbol appeared on her arm. So a challenge requiring a super effort was effective as a motivator. Some mediums carry on alarmingly in their efforts – Marthe Béraud, for example, sometimes looked as if she was wrestling with a difficult birth – while others, such as D D Home, seemed to be in a fairly placid state while rooms shook or the odd phantom crossed the room.

During a séance it is clear that the sitters in a circle have a marked effect on the strength and form taken by manifestations. The leader of a circle sitting with the Polish medium Kluski urged the sitters to help the medium by breathing in unison with him, with the result that an undersized materialised figure, i.e. a child-sized adult figure, increased in stature to almost full size. One of the leading members of Kluski's home circle happened to fix his attention and a soupçon of his imagination on a fur coat that was lying on the couch, whereupon it started to pulsate and resemble an animal rousing itself from sleep. A large snuffly doglike animal that licked hands and nosed in pockets was one of Kluski's occasionally materialised creatures and the sitter faced with an animated fur coat firmly closed the idea down, whereupon the fur coat settled back into its normal state (Weaver 2015).

Apart from contributions of physical power, the influence of expectation, belief and desire often has an obvious influence on what happens. The varying mediumship of Marthe Béraud was cited (in the article on the French connection) as an example of response to the expectations and desires of researchers – ectoplasm evolving into flesh and bone for the physiologist Richet, effigies that looked rather like papier maché for Schrenk-Notzing(who theorised about 'ideoplasty'), for her mentor Juliette Bisson anything from ectoplasm crawling snakelike over the medium's naked body, a fairy dancing on Mme Bisson's hand to a phantom figure of the deceased M. Bisson, and, for a hostile English committee, some minor effects. Her mediumship demonstrates plainly that people can exercise their contributions to psychic force to foster their chosen lines or to act as blockers.

Unlike most of us, mediums seem to have an especially permeable two-way channel between their conscious and their unconscious, and we have seen how some of their phenomena reflect closely the goals and desires of their sitters and researchers. But, in general, mediums who produce a variety of effects have little control over which effect is going to eventuate, and produce something rather than the very thing specified. The researchers with Eusapia Palladino might have asked for a table levitation, but instead had the stool pick itself up and place itself on the table. And, just as in the case of the floating letter, you don't always get what you want in the way that you wanted to get it. French researchers at the strictly scientific IMI must have been rather disconcerted by having to report to other scientists what happened at a séance with the Polish medium, Jan Guzik.

Guzik was known for his sensational materialisations, rather like those of Kluski, though he was a very different sort of person. He was an uneducated professional medium, well known for resorting to obviously fraudulent practices if given the freedom to do so, and he insisted on sitting in total darkness. The French scientists at the IMI took no chances: Guzik was stripped naked and sewn up in a catsuit, and had his hands held at all times, all of which must seriously have reduced his scope for fraud. Osty and his colleagues did not believe in Guzik's spirits, and wanted demonstrations of what they regarded as extended biology. They got it in a way they would hardly have wished for.

It started well. First they saw lights swirling around overhead. Then the lights formed pairs, and came a bit closer, and were seen to form pairs. These then clarified into pairs of eyes gazing earnestly at the sitters. As the sitters returned their gaze, faces began to form around the eyes, and the faces came closer, features sharpening. In the final stages, the faces, now heads rather than just faces, came right up to the sitters and planted rather moist kisses on their faces. I think it must have taken all the integrity of Osty and his colleagues to admit and report to their fellow scientists that they were being kissed by Guzik's spirit entities. This was not what they had wanted or would have requested, but it was very biological, and their unconscious gave them essentially what they had asked for (Osty 1926). The question is, does their experience indicate any general rule that can be applied to physical manifestations that take place when they are not present and not exerting any influence over those who are present?

By sprinkling carmine dye powder round and about, Crawford was able to show that ectoplasm was apparently issuing from, and returning to, what he calls the medium's trunk (he got his wife to examine Kathleen's stockings for traces of dye). This may have been reality for Crawford, but I don't see it as a universal model, and, even in the Goligher attic, I don't see it pushing the cavorting trumpet around. Even less can I imagine EB, trapped in polite conversation, exuding ectoplasm from various orifices to secure the letter he wanted to open and read – nor Home for that matter. As for Crookes's experiments with Home, I should say that psychic force there looks much more like an emission from the hand, linking it with hand passes appearing to give hypnotists power over their hypnotees. And the hand might be regarded as the baton of the mind that lies behind its gestures, because hands do not have power unless there is a mind behind the hand.

How do any of these models square with the full form materialisations of Crookes's other medium, Florence Cook? (And occasionally Home himself). If we are not very impressed by Florence, the more abundantly witnessed materialisations of Kluski and Indridi Indridison are very impressive, and they look more like Crawford's ectoplasm model. To my mind, the board experiments with Crookes and the materialised forms can both be covered by Crookes's psychic force if it is seen as a form of energy that can carry out simple psycho-kinetic tasks like board manipulation or the more complex actions like getting Home's accordion to play itself while dangled on its strap by a sitter or, more sensationally, while cruising around in mid-air; and, when psychic force is required to simulate human forms, my speculation is that it shapes itself accordingly and clothes its surfaces in material taken from the skin, hair and clothes of the medium and sitters, an opaque and skin-shell of a figure.

There is some support for this notion from the fact that materialisation is associated with reports of abraded clothing and the frequent observation of sitters that their hands and faces feel chilled. If particles are being removed from their surface I imagine sitters would feel like that, and perhaps this is why they report the impression of cold breezes. When Schrenck-Notzing collected some ectoplasm in a container, he was disappointed to find only traces of skin when the contents were examined, but this is not surprising if his medium had produced images of faces and hands. Losers of skin particles would not be aware of permanent loss (for there is no reason to expect this sort of borrowed material to be replaced), nor would anyone be aware of extra particles adding themselves to general household dust, but Kluski reported visible damage to the suits he wore during séances, noticing that they were becoming threadbare.

Ectoplasm is described as issuing from the medium's mouth, and, if the medium, sitters and researchers believe it to be some sort of substance originating inside the medium, it has to emerge from the medium's body by some plausible route. But if psychic force is more like a form of energy, it doesn't have to emerge from an orifice. Alfred Russel Wallace described ectoplasm appearing at the side of fully clothed medium F.W. Monck, looking as if it were emerging from between his ribs, though there was obviously no exit point there for any material substance. Continuing its unusual behaviour, the 'mist' took the shape of a twin personage, executed some dance movements together with its medium, and then dissolved back to a cloud of ectoplasm, dwindling to nothing as if re-entering the medium as it had emerged. This is closer to the concept of energy controlled by the medium and coating itself in particles. Monck, like most Victorian professional physical mediums, was reputed to be fraudulent, but perhaps not all the time. And Prof. Wallace was a distinguished man of science, not a fantasist.

Viewing psychic force as control of psi energy, it seems very relevant to the sphere of healing and medical hypnosis. The intended result of these two practices is the same, though they are not always bracketed together. When a medium/healer has a modifying effect on the body of a patient, is he doing something different from the actions of a hypnotist/healer? And are they both having a direct effect on the physiology or on the psychology of the patient? Probably the most astonishing cure verified in medical literature is the treatment by Dr Albert Mason of a young man with the dreadful 'crocodile skin' disease. By successive sessions of hypnosis he succeeded in clearing the patient's limbs of what he believed to be a serious infestation of warts, apparently effecting a permanent cure.

Then he learned that what he had cured was a form of ichthyosis, an incurable genetic disease. Even more extraordinary than the cure is that, on learning this, Mason lost his power to hypnotise and heal that patient, whose back remained covered with scales. If Mason had been a healer rather than a medical hypnotist, the effect on the patient would have been ascribed to some sort of influence, whether directly from the healer or from the healer's supposed spirits. Healing or hypnosis, the result would be the same. Healers and hypnotists both use suggestion, via words and gestures. Is there any good reason to ascribe one to psychic force but not the other?

When psychic force pushes down boards, or guides postal envelopes, a radiation model acting directly on things, whether wood or bodily tissue, seems very plausible, even if, as it was here, there was no immediate effect; the patient was told to come back the next week with one limb clear of the scales. A bombardment of psychic force delivered like radiotherapy may well take time to destroy its target, like a systemic weedkiller acting on roots.

But there is an alternative path to the results. Rather than the healer radiating forces to act on the patient's body tissues, Mason might have been hypnotically transmitting to the patient's mind a confidence in acting on his own physiology. A transmission of this sort might have been more in the nature of a telepathic command to the patient to clear the scales away, and, unlike Mason, or anyone else, the patient's unconscious might actually know the mechanics of how to remove ichthyosis scales from its own body, if enabled by psychic power to do so. Most healing takes place at close quarters, encouraging the concept of radiation acting on the patient's tissues; but when distant healing is taken into account then telepathic command to the mind of the patient is more plausible.

This leads to the very successful telepathic hypnosis experiments witnessed by Frederic Myers in France. The orders given to the servants in these hypnotic transmissions were nothing to do with healing, but the nature of the order is not the point. A command to open the window on a cold night might be because it would (however improbably) lead to an improvement in health rather than amount to an irrational action in response to an arbitrary hypnotic command. The effectiveness of these telepathic commands ties in with Dr Louisa Rhine's valuable observation that people who receive informational telepathic alerts seldom take action, attributing the information content to their own over-active imagination, but an unexplained command to drop everything and go somewhere or do something, unsupported by any reason, is much more likely to produce an immediate response. It is an order that must be acted on.

These unadorned telepathic summonses to action are never linked to hypnosis and still less to psychic force, which could be the initiator both of the volitionally delivered hypnosis and the unconsciously delivered telepathic summons or cry for help. Still less are healing cases related to PK or (in the case of remote healing) to distant hypnosis. And healing does look much more like cases of PK command/ telepathic hypnosis than the transmission of information, ideas or emotions, the usual subjects of telepathic resonance reports.

Let's take some form of telepathic PK further down the line, and even beyond organic systems, and ask if we can envisage the mind of D D Home exerting a similar sort of quasi-hypnotic influence on the minds, such as they might be, of the constituents of matter in the vicinity of the board, ordering their behaviour? Did EB's wish, to take hold of his letter, escape and be picked up by the 'minds' inherent in the stationery? Would that be in the molecules or in the entity constituting the letter-in-an-envelope? In posing these bizarre questions it is essential to bear in mind that whether or not conscious purposes are being realised, all psi output, as well as input, is effected by the powers of the unconscious mind, outside the control or awareness of the conscious person. The unawareness of the undoubted activator in poltergeist cases, next to be considered, clearly exemplifies this principle.

Poltergeists that manifest on a large scale, as in cases of bell-ringing and stone-throwing, usually have an unequivocal focus person whose presence initiates the outbreak and sustains it. One thing stands out as a fairly common factor: the focus person, however personally disturbed, is not doing anything deliberately to foment the disturbances, and may regard them with various degrees of dismay. Apart from the usual lack of conscious intention, how compatible are other features of poltergeist cases with the psychic force manifestions considered so far?

The Dixon belling-ringing case is one of the most vigorous ever reported in massive detail by a reliable observer, the friend of Myers who became a lifelong member of the SPR after writing his very circumstantial report. It will be remembered that the incidents started with the ringing of household bells from rooms all over the house when there was no one there to ring them. This was all before the days of household electricity, at a time when bells were activated by people pulling on a tassel hanging from the wall – not a bell push but a bell pull. Following the employment of fourteen-year-old Mary as maid of all work in Hugh Dixon's house, bells rang from unpeopled rooms, sometimes several at a time, causing the connecting cables to move, making familiar grinding noises as they rose through wooden joists and then fell back. The cables, in turn, pulled on clangers that rang in glass compartments arrayed on the walls of the kitchen passage, making numbers appear in the little windows indicating the rooms where the bells had been pulled. Later the more usual bangs, raps and furniture movements joined in the uproar. While this was going on, Mary could be observed from time to time by Dixon, cowering downstairs together with the terrified cook.

It was not just a case of a bell ringing at the end point; it would seem that (at least when under observation) every mechanical stage had been activated as if by invisible hands pulling on the bell tassels, even from a room where the tassel had come away from the wall so that there was nothing to pull. What sort of psychic force could have pulled bells and later done the usual banging around and furniture moving? There was nothing in the nature of ectoplasm around, and I think we can readily dismiss the idea of ectoplasm from Mary chasing around the house and pulling cables. Was she unconsciously emitting telepathic instructions to the minds/organising centres/nuclei of the constituents of the bell tassels telling them to pull themselves down, or perhaps telling cables to pull themselves up? In cases like this it is very plausible to invoke the participation of spirits to account for large-scale phenomena that seem beyond the reach of one disturbed mind. But, before giving up on human based psychic force, let us take a look at the largely overlooked manifestation of spatial discontinuity, otherwise known as jott.

Jott has already been quite broadly explored, and though its hallmark is its occurrence in the normal course of life, it does also feature frequently as an item among others in poltergeist cases. As a bridge between the rapids of poltergeist phenomena and the calms of jott, let us remember the stoning case of Tibor and Lazy in which the report writer Wratnik described the arrival of stones directed at Tibor when he was under observation. Wratnik said that he saw them materialising two or three feet away from Tibor. If they struck him, they did no injury because, though visible, they were not fully materialised, and if they were fully materialised before they reached him they plummeted to the ground, apparently unaffected by the propulsion of the partially materialised stone. This unique observation may have some relevance to the comings and goings of jott.

Jott also figures in materialisation sittings. I was told by witnesses to family séances held in the 1940s that sometimes when the materialisation session (involving deceased family members and friends) ended, a large bouquet of cut flowers was sometimes found on the hearth; inquiries of the local florist confirmed that on the following mornings the florists would often find flowers missing – but 'they' only took items that were surplus to arrangements, so it didn't matter!

The idea that all windfalls must have a corresponding flyaway does satisfy some sort of conservation of weirdness principle, and the coin that threw itself at Raymond Bayless's feet had presumably de-actualised from the display case of its owner. Did the psychic force emerge from the séance room and take itself down the road to the florists, and did Bayless leave some behind in the antique shop? Even if psychic force is imagined as a sort of diffusion rather than a focused spray (to apply crudely mechanistic concepts to a psi manifestation) we are a long way from ascribing that degree of psi power at a distance to frightened fourteen-year-old girls, or even stalwart landscape painters and mediums.

A telepathic network has been postulated, universal in some degree, but closely integrated between minds in resonance, on the same wavelength, so to speak. At closer quarters, let us bear in mind that sitters could contribute to Kluski's psi power by breathing in unison with him, so that his undersized materialisations could grow. Perhaps psi can draw on the potential power of others in their telepathic resonance group, so that they can actualise or de-actualise articles that are spatially remote but are within the reach of their amplified psychic force.

In an earlier article I proposed that PK, aka psychic force, initiated telepathy; that argument was based on the projection of telepathic command. When it comes to the transmission of knowledge, it becomes more evident that a signal must be conveying ideas: the fact, for example, that someone has died being an idea more than a compulsion to act, though it is still one that could be conveyed pictorially rather than by the use of language. If we are into the domain of awareness, we are into the realms of the immaterial thought, and we must face up to the familiar matter/mind question of how a physical force can impinge on insubstantial mental content, or vice-versa. The spatial anomalies that figured in the jott exposition prompted the same Cartesian impasse.

My preferred model to meet this problem is that mind and matter are not chalk and cheese, but two states of the same substance, which I call 'mindstuff.' (It has to be called something). According to the model, when the constituents of mindstuff are awake, they are in the mind state, and when they are asleep they are in the matter state, and always subject to the directions of those in the mind state. The two states are like water and ice, watery mind is alert, flowing and joined up; the mind-flow controls the movements of icebound, inert, isolated matter. Awake or asleep, it is the same substance, and can talk to itself.

Thinking mindstuff should present no problem to people (the majority) who have no difficulty in assuming that immaterial thoughts are generated by the electrical activity of the very material brain. It has to be admitted that there is so much correlation between brain and human functioning on every level that it may seem perverse not to regard it as being the mind itself, but telepathy and other psi powers seem to be outside the capacities of the brain. In support of the mind/brain non-identity it has been pointed out that though you don't receive a broadcast without a tuned circuit, the tuned circuit receiver is not actually creating the radio/TV programme; it is giving you access to it. We need the brain for access, and it has often been theorised that we need it as a filter, to admit only data relevant to our causal world, and to block the flood of telepathic data that would overwhelm us with confusion if it came up into consciousness.

The idea that consciousness is not necessarily seated in the coils of the brain is often associated with non-locality, a concept I do not understand, and – far from proposing it – I am about to launch into speculation about a cosmic mind, no less; and my concept of the great collective as a quasi-oceanic and all-embracing mind is definitely located in space/time, in that it occupies the whole of it, everything everywhere.

The ocean of mind is actually rather like ectoplasm, but instead of it emanating from humans, it consists of the mindstuff in which we and our world are immersed. It seems surprising that, in the midst of this inconceivable power, little drops in the ocean such as humans can exert an influence over our immediate vicinity; and, beyond that, send out attenuating ripples, ripples that can act on matter further afield and affect the movements and behaviour of matter there, if the action is ancillary to the area of main focus.

This sort of corruption of the causal reality is obviously an anomaly, and, bearing in mind the dwindling character of physical phenomena, it looks as if the system has repaired itself to the point of diminishing the frequency of conspicuously disruptive incidents. I suspect that the undermining of physical mediumship, especially where volitional but also where unsought (as in poltergeist attraction) has been effected by turning the zeitgeist against physical manifestations, largely by stigmatising them as scientifically impossible, offence against science being the new sacrilege. In the research field, mediumship has been degraded by furthering the Rhine doctrine that séances belong in the Victorian era and the future lies in showing that we all have a little bit of psi that can be demonstrated by statistical evaluation. There is nothing disruptive about that; it looks almost like science. In a telepathically interconnected world the zeitgeist can be expected to play a significant role in steering things this way or that, and that is the preferred direction.

Back to the Cosmic Mind – in its integrated state, the Cosmic Mind, like all minds, has a centre of being but it does not play an active role in managing the drama in which we are at the same time observers, players and occasional improvisers, because the owner of a mind largely dissociated into sub-entities (and sub-sub entities), is mostly in a suspended state of awareness. But, whether we are awake, asleep, comatose or dissociated, our autonomic system continues to regulate our functions so as to keep things going in good order; so does the global control mechanism of the Cosmic Mind – the control tells its oceanic constituents how to configure matter so as to maintain a comprehensible environment.

By comprehensible I mean that, so far as our world is concerned, everything that exists, or appears to exist, and everything that happens, must be consistent with what immediately preceded it, so that you can fairly predict what is about to happen and not suffer a shock by finding that it didn't happen. If you are driving a car you don't want to find, suddenly, that you are riding a bicycle. That would be as bewildering as being in a dream where anything might happen for no apparent reason. So the control has one ruling principle, the default causality directive, which is to ensure the consistency of one moment to another. Whether or not things happen one after another because of causation or because they merely succeed one another in an order that looks causal, matters to the argument not at all, so long as the result is sequential.

My conjecture is that the default causality directive is dinned into the unconscious minds of all the sentient entities that make up the totality of global creation, and the more substantial the mind receiving its instructions, the more responsibility it has to maintain order. When presenting the small theory of everything I argued, and still think plausible, that it is the function of our telepathic 'circuits' to receive instructions as to how to order the oceanic matter to remain in a state of actualisation consistent with its preceding state, and to alter its configuration in accordance with the script in each succeeding moment, and that we do this by psychic force, this being what our psychokinetic powers are for.

Misuse of the telepathic receptors leads to breakdown in the psychic force that ought to be upholding the fabric of our immediate environment – careless actualisation resulting in unsought jott and even more unsought poltergeist effects, while wilful misuse opens the door to the fantasies of the séance room. So, failure to maintain sequential stability leads to the raw material of psychical research, the precious by-product of psychic disobedience giving us access to the forbidden fruit of psychic force. By such unscheduled pathways we give ourselves glimmerings of advance insight into the forbidden knowledge, the greater reality behind our orderly little world.

ENVOI

⁓

It will have been evident to the perfect reader, starting at page 1 and continuing, rapt and attentive, to the final thoughts on psychic force, that, to a large extent, I have been saying the same things, with some variations, for the last thirtyrty years or so, and while that repetition may be fully justified as years roll by and people forget, dismiss or ignore what they may have heard years before, it may be something of an irritant if they encounter the same idea several times within one week. *Mea culpa.*

The small theory of everything, which (like the dissertation on proof) originated many years ago, included most of the ideas, while the last talk, re-stating a lot of that material, was delivered much more recently. Some of the repeated argument has been removed or summarized, but in other ways themes have been amplified, adding some ideas to those already formed when the small theory originated.

People theorizing in most fields are motivated, on one hand to prise threads apart for examination, and on the other hand to pull threads together. Looking back, I like to think that I have drawn PK, Dmils, healing and hypnosis into the embrace of psychic force, and linked psychic force with telepathic reception, thus covering the spatial field of psychic phenomena in a unified system. I would like to have been able to present a great unified theory embracing ideas compatible with things as they are or seem to be, but realistically I have to settle for the presentation of some suggestive propositions.

Readers may wonder what is the significance of that seemingly irrelevant word 'spatial.' There is one powerful aspect of psi that is not included in the synthesis of psychic force/telepathy, and that is clairvoyance. It was back in the early 1970s that I was first bowled over by the clairvoyance of Stefan Ossowiecki, and realised that his sightings of the past, the video-like replay of scenes associated with the targets, pointed to clairvoyance being effected by retrocognition, implying the persistence of the past (the past including everything that does not lie in the future). That strikes me as a very significant implication. This is psi operating through time rather than space.

An idea that has originated in more recent years would, if well founded, unify to some extent normal and paranormal under one universal principle, that principle being probability law. I used the word 'directive' in connection with sequential causality, a directive being something that ought to be complied with but can, in fact, be disobeyed. Probability is conceived as an absolute law embracing normal and paranormal under its all-embracing curve, the graphic curve below which lies every possibility. At the immensely high apex of this curve are normal, almost inevitable, sequential events; trailing away at its remotest fringes lie improbable events, psi events being the most improbable.

This means that if we go through a period, such as the 100 years starting around 1840, when a lot of highly improbable paranormal incidents occurred, probability law will assert itself by balancing it with a period in which the zeitgeist militates against psi, and those massive effects will diminish, leaving a little jott to rear its unobtrusive head above the parapet from time to time, and occasionally some more conspicuous effects such as those credited to 'psychic detectives' assisting the American police, so long as their assistance is called detection and not retrocognition. Sadly, we have all too much evidence for the decline of mediumship. I find it quite satisfying to blame that on the laws of probability, because the same laws may one day lead to another golden age of psi.

The End

REFERENCES

~

Barrington M. R., Stevenson I. and Weaver Z. (2005) *A World in a grain of sand*, Mc.Farland & Company, Inc.

Barrington M. R., Mulacz P. and Rivas, T. (2005) 'Iris Farczady: a stolen life'. JSPR 69, 49-77

Barrington M. R . (1965, 19691976) 'The case of the flying thermometer', JSPR 43, 11-20, 45, 149-161, 48, 11-20.

Do. (1992) 'Franek Kluski, Psi Resarcher' 5,7,8.

Do. (1998), 'Jott: an extraordinary case of trade-in', PR 5, p.54

Do. (2011) 'A slip in time and space', PR 58

Do. (2012) 'The Nikolsburg poltergeist', PR 62

Do. (2018 *Jott: when things disappear...and then come back or relocate - and why it really happens*, Anomalist Books.

Barrett W. F. (1918) Report of physical phenomena taking place at Belfast with Dr. Crawford's medium, PSPR 30, 334-337

Bayless R. (1972) *Experiences of a Psychical Researcher*, Lyle Stuart, USA

Bem D. J. (2011) 'Feeling the future', Personality and social psychology.

Bem D. J. et al. (2016) 'Feeling the Future' 'Feeling the Future Metalevel' pdf

Bender H. (1969) 'New developments in poltergeist research', Proceedings of the Parapsychological Association, 6, 81.

Bisson, J. A. (1914) *Les phénomènes dits de matérialisation*, Alcan, Paris

Carrington H. (1930) *The Story of Psychic Science*, Rider & Co.

Do. (1952) *Psychic Oddities*, Rider & Co.

Cay B. M. W. (1992) 'Two transient documents', SPRJ 58, 232

Crawford, W. J. (1919) *The Reality of Psychic Phenomena*, John M. Watkins.

Do. (1919) *Experiments in Psychical Science*, John M. Watkins.

Do. (1921) *Psychic Structures at the Goligher Circle*, John M. Watkins

Eyesenck H. J. (1972) *Astrology: Science or Superstition?* Temple Smith

Flournoy, T. (1900) *Des Indes à la planète Mars*, Eggiman, Geneva

Geley G. (1927) *Clairvoyance and Matérialisation* (trans. Stanley de Brath), T. Fisher, Unwin, trans. by Stanley de Brath from *Materialisation et clairvoyance*, Paris, Alcan.

Gregory A. Ed. (1982) 'London experiments with Matthew Manning', PSPR 56, 284-365.

Hamilton T. (2017) *Arthur Balfour's ghosts*, Exeter UK, Imprint Academic.

Haraldsson E and Ggissurarson L. R (2015) *Indridi Indridison: The Icelandic Physical Medium*, White Crow Books

Iredell D. (1986) 'Letter to the editor', SPRJ, 53, 401-403

Jinks, T. (2016) *Disappearing object phenomenon: An investigation*, McFarland & Company, Inc.

Jung C.G. (2005) *Memories, Dreams, Reflections*, Fontana Press, original 1962, *Erinnerungen, Träume, Gedanken*, Rascher, Zürich.

Mason A. A. (1952) 'A case of congenital ichthyosiform erythrodermia of Brocq treated by hypnosis', British Medical Journal 2,4781 (August 23, 1952) 422-3

Murray G. (1916/18) 'Presidential Address' 1915, PSPR 29, 2-63, and see Verrall, Mrs. A.W. (1916) A series of experiments in "guessing," PSPR 29, 64-110

Medhurst R. G. ed.,(1972) *Crookes and the spirit world*, Souvenir Press.

Méheust, B. (2005) *Un clairvoyant prodigieux: Alexis Didier 1826-1886*, Les Empêcheurs de penser en rond.

Do. (1995) *Somnambulism et mediumnité,* (tome 2) Les Empêcheurs de penser en rond.

Myers, F. W. H. (1886) 'Human Personality in the light of Hypnotic Suggestion', PSPR, 4, 1-24.

Do. (1886) 'Telepathic hypnotism, and its relation to other forms of hypnotic suggestion', PSPR, 4, 127-188.

Do. (1896/7) 'The subliminal self', PSPR 11, 334-593, 395-401.

Osty, E. (1922) "Un Fait de Préconnaissance du Devenir de la Personnalité humaine", Revue Métapsychique 1922/3,204-207

Do. (1923) *Supernormal Faculties in Man,* (trans. Stanley de Brath) Methuen & Co

Do. (1927) 'Une utilisation pratique de la connaissance supranormale', Revue Métapsychique   1927/4, 238, 244.

Do. (1929) Guzik at the IMI' Revue Métapsychique 1929/6 and see Par. Rev. Archives 62 and 64.

Owen I. M. and A. R. G. Owen, 'Teleportation', New Horizons, 18.

Playfair G. L (2002) *Twin Telepathy: The Psychic Connection,* Vega, London.

Poynton J. C. (1975) (Ed) 'Parapsychology in South Africa', South African Society for Psychical Research.

Prince, M. (1978) *The Dissociation of a Personality,* Oxford University Press, (original edition 1905)

Prince W. F. (1964) *The Case of Patience Worth,* Virginia, University Books.

Report (1922) 'Report on a Series of Sittings with Eva C'., P SPR, 32, 209-343.

Rhine L. E. (1981) *The Invisible Picture,* McFarland & Company, Inc.

Richet C. (1923) *Thirty Years of Psychical Research* translated from (1994) *Traité de Métapsychique, Artha Productions,* first published 1922.

Roy A. E. (1990) *A sense of Something Strange,* Dog and Bone.

Schrenck-Notzing, A. von (1923) *Phenomena of Materialisation,* Kegan Paul, trans. By E.E. Fournier d,Albe from (1913) Materialisations Phänomene, Reinhardt, Munich.

Sheldrake R. (1999) *Dogs That Know When Their Owner is Coming Home and Other Unexplained Powers of Animals*, Arrow Books, and see commentary on a paper by Wiseman, Smith and Milton on the 'psychic pet' phenomenon, JSPR 63, 306-311

Sidgwick Mrs. H, (1888) On the evidence for premonitions, PSPR, 5, 288-354.

Smith, Whately W. (1918/19) "The reality of psychic phenomena", PSPR 30, 306-333

Stevenson I. (1970) *Telepathic impressions*: a Review and Report on 35 New Cases, University of Virginia Press.

Sudre R, (1956) Traité de Parapsychologie, Editions Payot, Paris, 1960, trans. C.E. Green, George Allen & Unwin.

Warcollier René, 1940-1946, Un cas de changement de personnalité avec xénoglossie. La Métapsychique, 1940-1946/1 pp.121-129

Weaver Z. (2015) *Other realities? The enigma of Franek Kluski's mediumship*, White Crow Books.

Key to abbreviations

SPR	SPR Journal
PSPR	SPR Proceedings
Psi Res.	Psi Researcher
Para. Rev.	Paranormal Review

All are available via the SPR On-line library.

INDEX OF NAMES

~

www.ingramcontent.com/pod-product-compliance
Lightning Source LLC
Chambersburg PA
CBHW020154090426
42734CB00008B/811